Be a Saint in the Making

The Family Consecration to the Immaculate Heart of Mary through the Intercession of Saint Carlo Acutis

Kristi Dentinger

En Route Books and Media, LLC
Saint Louis, MO

⚓ENROUTE
Make the time

En Route Books and Media, LLC
5705 Rhodes Avenue
St. Louis, MO 63109

FRONT COVER:
Be a Saint in the Making with the Immaculate Heart of Mary
and the Intercession of Saint Carlo Acutis, image copyright 2025
by Goretti Fine Art. All rights reserved. Used with permission.
Gorettifineart.com

PAGE 36:
Image, "Lo, I Am With You Always" by Traci Douglass.
All rights reserved. Used with permission. Tracidouglass.com

ISBN-13: 979-8-88870-444-8 and 979-8-88870-467-7
Library of Congress Control Number: 2025948133

Visit the Real Presence Education Foundation (RPEF)
online at https://realpresence-edu.org/

BE A SAINT IN THE MAKING has received an Imprimatur: In accordance
with CIC 827, permission to publish has been granted on August 5, 2025,
by the Most Reverend Mark S. Rivituso, Archbishop-Designate of Mobile, AL.
Permission to publish is an indication that nothing contrary to Church teaching
is contained in this work. It does not imply any endorsement of the opinions
expressed in the publication; nor is any liability assumed by this permission.

ENDORSEMENTS

"Today, more than ever, the domestic church of the family is key to the success of passing on the faith to the next generation of Catholics. *Be a Saint in the Making* is a practical and meaningful aid to parents who want to raise their children in the spiritual traditions of our Church. It helps us to recognize that saintliness is in the reach of every person, no matter their age. As a pastor, I count a resource like this as a most valuable companion to families in the advancement of holiness of life."

– Rev. Matthew O'Toole, Pastor St. Peter Church

"*Be a Saint in the Making* is a beautiful and timely book that brings faith to life in a relatable way. I especially appreciated the emphasis on the story of Blessed Carlo Acutis—his love for the Eucharist, his everyday holiness, and his passion for using his talents to serve God make him a remarkable role model for young people today. The book reminds us that sainthood is not distant or unattainable—it is a universal call. Equally valuable are the weekly activities designed for families. They are simple, engaging, and provide meaningful opportunities to pray, serve, and grow together in faith without feeling overwhelming. If you are seeking a resource that will inspire your children—and you—to see sainthood as both possible and joyful, this book is an excellent choice. It is uplifting, encouraging, and a wonderful tool for families desiring to deepen their relationship with God."

– St. Peter parishioner, a participant in the pilot

"*Be a Saint in the Making* beautifully equips families to consecrate themselves to the Immaculate Heart of Mary with Saint Carlo Acutis as guide, offering a practical, prayerful path to holiness through Scripture, devotion, and daily love."

– Dr. Sebastian Mahfood, OP, author of *The Narrative Spirituality of Dante's Divine Comedy*

BE A SAINT IN THE MAKING has received an Imprimatur: In accordance with CIC 827, permission to publish has been granted on August 5, 2025, by the Most Reverend Mark S. Rivituso, Archbishop-Designate of Mobile, AL. Permission to publish is an indication that nothing contrary to Church teaching is contained in this work. It does not imply any endorsement of the opinions expressed in the publication; nor is any liability assumed by this permission.

Consecrate your family to the Immaculate Heart of Mary with the intercession of Saint Carlo Acutis. "Be a Saint in the Making" is a 16 week family consecration movement following the first five Saturdays requested by Our Lady of Fatima along with the first millennial Saint, Saint Carlo Acutis.

"Find God and you will find the meaning of your life...God has written an unique and unrepeatable story for each of us, but he lets us write the ending."
- Saint Carlo Acutis

Join us on this journey to be Saints in the making. Find God's Heart, within the Immaculate Heart of Mary, and with it, find the meaning of your life. With the intercession of Saint Carlo Acutis, write the unique and unrepeatable story of your family's journey to holiness, to join all the Saints in Heaven as one Holy Family of God, royal sons and daughters. God's heart is waiting to hear the fiat of "yes" from your heart. He desires all to be Saints. The end is yours to write!

TABLE OF CONTENTS

INTRODUCTION

God is perfect in love and in mercy. His very essence is love. God's mercy to all is the perfection of his love for all. He is truly holy. God created each of us to be holy, as he is Holy, to love as he loves. He desires that we are who he meant us to be, saints with a capital "S", holy in love. In Baptism we become a child of God, receiving his life and graces to become holy, to be Saints with the help of the fire of his Spirit, the fire of his cross, the fire of his love, which he freely gives to all who ask.

God wants us to strive for holiness, to love as he loves. But what does this striving look like? St. Therese of Lisieux says, *"Holiness consists simply in doing God's will, and being just what God wants us to be."* Her words have a beautiful simplicity to them, however, it can still seem out of reach for many living a busy family life outside of a convent.

God wills only our good. He is all good and all loving! God desires for all of his children to be holy. He is always calling souls and giving them the grace to fulfill who they were meant to be, making them Saints— to love as he loves.

Pope St. John Paul II, at World Youth day in Santiago, Spain in 1989, shared this encouraging message with all those in attendance, *"Do not be afraid to be holy! Have the courage and humility to present yourselves to the world determined to be holy, since full, true freedom is born from holiness."*

"Holiness is the perfection of love"
— St. Thomas Aquinas.

ST. CARLO ACUTIS

St. Carlo Acutis was not afraid to be holy, to love as God loves. He is the first millennial Saint. His original canonization, postponed due to the death of Pope Francis, was scheduled to be held on April 27th, 2025, Divine Mercy Sunday. It is not a coincidence that this is the feast day of God's love and mercy for us. Saint Carlo Acutis had the courage and determination to be holy, to love as God loves, in our present age. Pope Francis shared in a youth synod at the Vatican in 2019 these words about then Blessed Carlo Acutis, "Carlo didn't fall into the trap. He saw that many young people, wanting to be different, really end up being like everyone else, running after whatever the powerful set before them with the mechanisms of consumerism and distraction. In this way they do not bring forth their gifts the Lord has given them; they do not offer the world those unique personal talents that God has given to each of them. As a result, Carlo said, 'everyone is born as an original, but many people end up dying as photocopies.' Don't let that happen to you!"

Starting at the very young age of three, Carlo seemed determined to be who God wanted him to be, to use his gifts to be a Saint. Over the short fifteen years of his life, he chose to love, to live his life for God. He developed and brought forth his gifts that the Lord had given him in many unique ways, according to God's plan and path of holiness for him. Carlo is quoted as saying that "to be close to Jesus, that's my life plan." He lived this plan of holiness, of love, not on his own strength but with the help of grace.

Grace is the gifts of the Holy Spirit in our lives to make us Holy. The Holy Spirit gave Mary the gift of an Immaculate Heart from her conception to love as God loves. She desires to share this gift with us. As our own Mother she gives us Her Heart to help us to be Holy, to be Saints, and lead us to Jesus her son and to His Sacred Heart, to love as he loves.

At the request of Jesus, spoken from the cross, St. John took Mary into his home as his mother. She shared the gift of her Immaculate Heart with him. St. John sat at her feet, as Jesus had sat at her feet, and he learned how to be holy, how to love as God loves, to be set apart for God's will, to be who he was meant to be, a Saint.

Jesus asks all of us to take His Mother into our homes, for her to be with us in the midst of our family life, the domestic church, teaching us how to love as God loves. He desires that we sit at her feet and learn to be holy. It was God's will that she, with St. Joseph, created the perfect, loving, holy family life for Jesus to grow up in, the first domestic church. "And when they had performed everything according to the law of the Lord, they returned into Galilee, to their own city, Nazareth. And the child grew and became strong, filled with wisdom; and the favor of God was upon him." (Luke 2:39-40)

THE BLESSED MOTHER

*C*arlo, as a child, grew in holiness with the help of the Blessed Mother. In her book, *My Son Carlo*, the mother of St. Carlo Acutis, Antonia, shares a vision he received as a young child. "Another time, when he was around eight, he saw Our Lady of Fatima during a procession in church. She stopped in front of him and gave him her heart. She placed it in his chest. She told him to consecrate himself to her Immaculate Heart and to the Sacred Heart of Jesus."

Carlo responded to Our Lady's request, which was God's will for him, with his fiat of "yes" and consecrated himself to her Immaculate Heart to learn to love as God loves. He was very devoted to her and said, "Each time that we address the Mother of God, we place ourselves in direct and immediate contact with Heaven. It is almost as if we enter. In calling her 'full of grace', in invoking her in this manner, we attest to our filial faith. We believe in her in this way. We hope that she is the giver of all things good. Of every Grace. We say, 'Pray for us'- that is, we invite her to use her status to meet us halfway. We address her knowing that she is Omnipotentia Supplex (omnipotent for intercession). Her intercession is assured. Her intervention is taken for granted. Her prayer is infallible. The human race, through Mary, was given a supernatural dignity. God associated himself with a creature, a mother. A mystery!"

The Blessed Mother responded to God's will for her, to his love and plan, with her fiat of "yes". In all of her daily activities, in the domestic church of her home, God made her into who she was meant to be, the Holy Mother of God. Give your Fiat and say "Yes" to Jesus, to love all around you as he loves, with the Consecration of your family to the Immaculate Heart of Mary. Within her heart and with the intercession of Saint Carlo Acutis you are invited to "be a Saint in the making" as they lead your family into holiness, into a more intimate, loving, union with the Sacred Heart of Jesus, our Lord and Savior, *the King of Love.*

STEPS OF CONSECRATION

*I*talian Cardinal Carlo Caffarra, received a letter in the 1980's from Fatima Visionary, Sister Lucia. She told him: "Father, a time will come when the decisive battle between the Kingdom of Christ and Satan will be over marriage and family. And those who work for the good of the family will experience persecution and tribulation. But do not be afraid, because Our Lady has already crushed his head." Many families are currently experiencing this battle, but Our Lady of Fatima has a battle plan!

Sister Lucia shared this battle plan with Saint Carlo Acutis: "A few days after the death of Sister Lucia in 2005, Carlo dreamed of her. She told him that the practice of the first five Saturdays of the month could change the destiny of the world," Antonia, "My Son Carlo."

In a 1930 apparition, Jesus revealed to Sister Lucia,

The reason for the five Saturdays of the month is simple, it is because there are five types of offenses and blasphemies against the Immaculate Heart of Mary:

1) Blasphemies against Her Immaculate Conception.

2) Blasphemies against her Perpetual Virginity.

3) Blasphemies against her Divine Motherhood, in refusing Mary's Spiritual Motherhood for all God's people.

4) Blasphemies of those who seek to sow in the hearts of children indifference, scorn, or even hatred of this Immaculate Mother.

5) Offenses of those who dishonor and outrage her directly in Her Holy images.

Appearing to Lucia, in 1943, Jesus declared,

"I desire most ardently the propagation of the cult of the devotion to the Immaculate Heart of Mary, because the love of this Heart attracts souls to Me, it is the center from which the rays of My light and My love go through all the earth, and the unquenchable fountain from which the living water of My mercy flows into the earth."

THE FIRST FIVE SATURDAYS OF THE MONTH

Consecrating to the Immaculate Heart of Mary allows for the ultimate flow of Jesus' light, peace, love, and mercy, into our hearts, into our families.

This consecration follows the Devotion of the first five Saturdays of the month, as requested by Our Lady of Fatima.

Our Lord, speaking again to Lucia in 1930, clarified the devotion saying, "This Communion will be accepted on the following Sunday for just reasons, if my Priests allow it so." Acting in reparation, for the blasphemies and offenses to her Immaculate Heart, we will repair on the first Saturday or Sunday, if necessary, for five consecutive months by:

1) Receiving Holy Communion

2) Confession (can be within 8 days before or after)

3) Praying 5 decades of the Rosary

4) Keeping her company by meditating, for 15 additional minutes, on Mysteries of the Rosary*

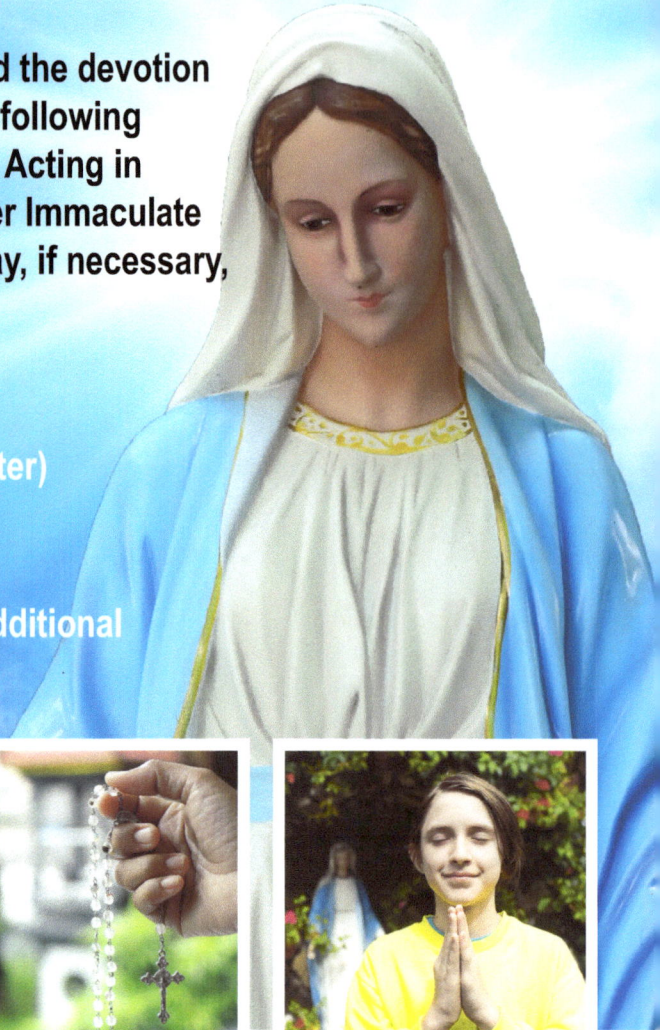

This workbook contains 16 weeks of simple, easy activities for busy families to grow in holiness with the intercession of Saint Carlo Acutis. Starting each week, take one thing from the reflection for your weekly journey. Included are a daily prayer and a Bible Scripture; try memorizing for a challenge! Each week contains a fun family activity. Choose from the list of the Holy Habits. A colorful graph is provided, helping your family keep track of their steps towards consecration.

Our Lady of Fatima promised, "In the end, my Immaculate Heart will triumph!" Consecrating our families to her, let's join her triumphant battle plan, changing the destiny of the world, one family at a time, beginning with us!

*helpful sites: rosarycenter.org, mariavision.us, intothedeep.com

HOLY SACRIFICE OF THE MASS

On the journey to the King, we are invited and can travel daily to Mass, where Heaven comes down, joined to earth. Coming before the God of all creation, we gather around him, worshipping in adoration with all the Saints and Angels. Encounter, in the Mass, the Mystery of perfect Love made Flesh, the Word of God, for our salvation. Share in the Last Supper of our Lord, the family meal of his Holy Sacrifice for our redemption. Prepare, beforehand, to receive the graces, the gifts of the Holy Spirit, of this Most Sacred Mystery of God's love and mercy, making us into Saints. Open your hearts, in thanksgiving, to prepare for the Holy Sacrifice of the Mass, to receive the King of Love in the Eucharist — Greek for Thanksgiving. Your bodies dressed for an audience with the King of the Universe!

Entering the Church, bless yourself and your children, with Holy Water. Making the sign of the Cross, renew your Baptism and call to be Saints as beloved children of God, members of the royal family of God! As a sign of reverence, in his royal court, the Church of God, bow or genuflect, on the right knee, before the Tabernacle and when entering or exiting the pew. The Priest, "in persona Christi," invites us to enter into the presence of the Holy Trinity by signing ourselves with the sign of the Cross, our protection and salvation. The Introductory Rites, the prayers at the beginning of Mass, are where we, in giving our responses; enter into a dialogue with the Holy Trinity, our intentions rising to Heaven as a prayer. We commune in a prayerful, harmonious symphony, as a family, acknowledging our sins, and asking for forgiveness as we confess to God and to each other. With the Priest, we receive forgiveness from God.

Communing together, we are before the King of Heaven and earth, gathered before the altar, the symbol of Jesus in his offering on the Cross. He is present, giving us his heart. Make a throne in your heart for him, by singing to him from your heart! Listen with your hearts to the readings, the Word of God. Let them set your hearts on fire, as Jesus did with the disciples on the road to Emmaus, opening their hearts to receive Him in the first Eucharist after he rose from the dead. Profess your faith with the creed. Unite yourself to the Priest as he begins the consecration at the altar, for at your baptism you were anointed priest, prophet and king. Send your guardian angel along with the offering, placing your petitions, your gifts, your heart, your thanksgiving to God upon the altar. Listen to the prayers, spoken during the consecration at the altar, and you will know the faith of the church, your faith.

During the consecration upon the altar, the painful, life-giving sacrifice of Jesus as High Priest, Prophet and King of Kings is the pure Sacrifice for our sins, Blood and Water pouring down. The Holy Offering as the Lamb of God, the Essence of pure Love and full obedience to God the Father, takes place perpetually in Heaven, on earth, on the altar. Jesus, transformation of bread into Body, wine into Blood, is incarnate by the Holy Spirit and the efficacious words of the Priest "in persona Christi." This is Who we receive, on our tongue, on our knees, when in grace we receive the Holy Eucharist. Receiving Eternal Love and Mercy, Heaven on earth - Divinity - God himself, divinizing his royal children, his holy family of love. The timeless sacrifice of Jesus takes place on every altar, at every Mass, in every Catholic Church. Worship and adore him, in your hearts with love and thanksgiving, for he gives ALL, every moment, every time, we come before him to celebrate the Holy Sacrifice of the Mass.

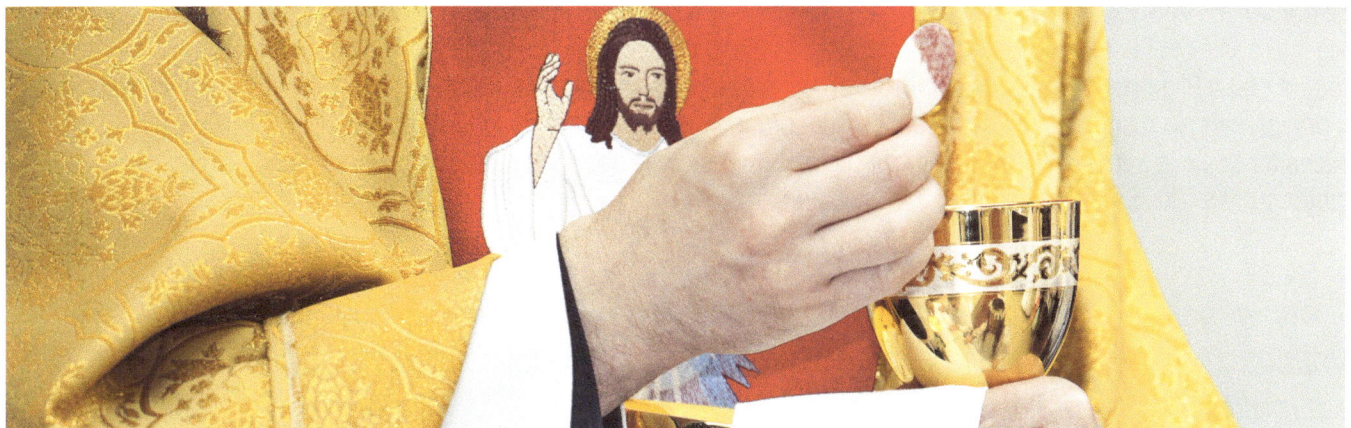

HOLY HABITS

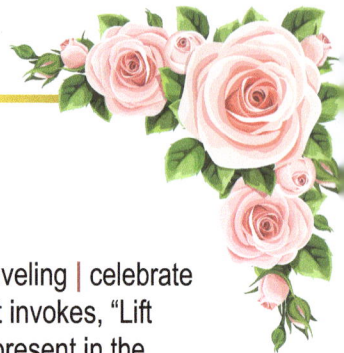

ROSES IN SPITE OF DAILY THORNS

Mass — After Mass talk about "one take away" | attend Mass every Sunday, even when traveling | celebrate Mass at Church dedicated to a Saint on their feast day | during the consecration, when the Priest invokes, "Lift up your hearts" whisper to children: "Here we go up to Heaven!"(Dr. Scott Hahn) | talk to Jesus, present in the Tabernacle, worshipped and adored by angels surrounding him | "pray Mass" for an intention or desire | receive Jesus on tongue | after receiving Jesus in the Holy Eucharist speak to him with love from your heart, thanking him and praising him | greet Jesus when kneeling down before Mass, listen in the silence of your heart waiting for a whisper or nudge from his heart | make the sign of the cross when driving by a Catholic Church, Jesus is in the Tabernacle

Morning — Pray the Angelus | morning offering | when riding to school have passenger read daily readings | listen to the Divine office on "SingtheHours.com" | read the Bible every day, even for 5 minutes | have a designated prayer area/altar in house | hang a crucifix in every bedroom, making sign of cross with Holy Water or blessed oil | dedicate each month to a Saint and Spiritual gift | start a family journal of everyday miracles, revisiting to see how God is providing for your family | wear a brown scapular or medal | pray "Hail Mary" when hear a siren | Guardian Angel prayer

Afternoon — Pray the Angelus | learn a verse from Scripture or Catechism, receive a treat from goody basket | Scripture quizzes/contests with each other from Bible websites or Hallow app | Eucharistic Adoration, even for 15 minutes | kit for children to play the Mass/Stations of the Cross | daily rosary~ each child leading a different decade | celebrate Saints feast days for each family member | celebrate Baptism day as big as birthday | pray the Rosary with 10 felt roses and a statue of Mary ~ place a felt rose at the feet of Mary after each "Hail Mary" | pray "Hail Mary" when stopped at a yellow/red light

Evening — Pray the Angelus | share "roses and thorns" of the day as a mini examin, praying the Divine Mercy Chaplet for all intentions | read daily Gospel before meal prayer | each share a prayer or intention for another family member, children taking turns leading the family prayer | read a book about Saints before bed or meals | "Hail Mary, Gentle Woman" as bedtime song | pray three "Hail Marys" for purity | watch episodes of Chosen | learn and live the Spiritual and corporal works of Mercy | prayer of thanksgiving to God for your day

General — Ask for blessing from Our Lady of Highway when traveling | pray Guardian Angel prayer when getting into a vehicle | keep your families hearts holy on Sundays and Holy Days | Holy Water fonts vicinity of bedrooms | take Pilgrimages to Shrines, family cemeteries and other Catholic Churches | grace before meal and after meal prayer, even in restaurants | be present in the moment ~ giving full attention to the other person | offer up little sacrifices for souls in purgatory | smile and compliment others | only allow yourself one hour a week on social media/computer games (like Saint Carlo Acutis)

Visit our website, BeASaintInTheMaking.com, for a longer list of Holy Habits & Devotions practiced by families in their everyday journey to holiness, to be Saints in the making.

Carlo's Holiness Kit

- Love God with all your heart
- Go to Mass
- Receive Communion
- Pray the Rosary
- Read a passage of the Bible
- Visit Jesus in the Tabernacle
- Go to confession monthly*
- Help others as much as you can
- Rely on your guardian angel as your best friend

* Carlo went weekly

	MASS	FAMILY ROSARY	CONFESSION	VISIT JESUS	FAMILY ACTIVITY	HOLY HABIT	HELPING & MAKING SACRIFICES	PRAYER/ SCRIPTURE
1ST SATURDAY								
WEEK 2								
WEEK 3								
WEEK 4								
2ND SATURDAY								
WEEK 2								
WEEK 3								
WEEK 4								
3RD SATURDAY								
WEEK 2								
WEEK 3								
WEEK 4								
4TH SATURDAY								
WEEK 2								
WEEK 3								
WEEK 4								
5th Saturday				Consecrate your family to the Immaculate Heart of Mary				

BE A SAINT

"You, too, can be a saint, but you need to want it with your whole heart, and if you don't have a desire for it right now, ask the Lord for it, and you will see, He will give it to you." – Saint Carlo Acutis

Carlo Acutis was born on May 3rd, 1991 into an Italian family. He lived for most of his life in Milan, Italy with his parents Andrea Acutis and Antonia Salzano Acutis. Peering into his life from the outside, he looked like any other typical child. He loved to play soccer. He had pets: four dogs, two cats and numerous goldfish. He loved to play on his PlayStation. He would hang out with his many friends and use his cellphone. He learned to play the saxophone and had a sweet tooth. But in many ways he was not a typical child, nor were his parents a typical Catholic family.

Usually, it is the parents who pass down their Catholic faith to their children. In the case of Carlo, he passed his faith onto his parents. His mother, Antonia, says that before Carlo she had only been to Mass for her First Communion, her Confirmation and her wedding. His father's faith was not much stronger. Antonia shared about Carlo that, "I was perplexed by his devotion.. he was so small and so sure."

It was Beata, their devoted Polish nanny, who first lit the fire of God's love in his heart. Antonia has said that "Beata was one of the first people to speak to Carlo about God." It was she who took him to his first Mass. It would have been Beata who sowed little seeds of faith into Carlo's heart, in the domestic church of his first few years of life with his family.

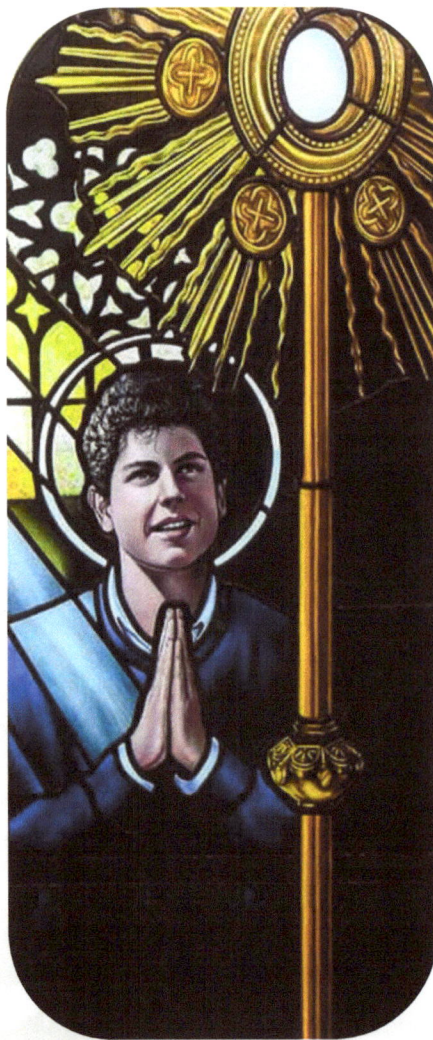

Antonia has remarked that "He was three or four years old when he started asking very deep questions. He was very attracted to the church, Jesus and the Virgin Mary." It was Beata who would have answered these early deep questions from her own faith and love for God, awakening his soul to God's love.

God, in his perfect will, chose Andrea and Antonia to be Carlo's parents. He does not make mistakes. He knew that they would be the perfect family to have a special child that showed a burning desire to love God at a very young age. God gave them the desire to help Carlo be who he was meant to be, a Saint; and in the process, they also found their own faith and burning desire to love God as he loves.

Will you respond, as Carlo's family did, to God's call, to be holy and ask for a burning desire to love him as he loves and be holy as he is holy, to be a Saint?

TOGETHER WE PRAY . . .

Lord, We desire, with all our hearts, to become holy, to be Saints with a capital "S." Please give us the fire of the Holy Spirit, the fire of your Cross, and the fire of your Love. Make us, we pray, into who we are meant to be as your royal sons and daughters. We ask this in the name of Jesus. Amen

FAMILY ACTIVITY

We are all Saints in the making! God desires each child to be a Saint. He gave each of us unique gifts of the Spirit for our path to holiness, to love as he loves. Each child is unique and uniquely loved by God. Each Saint is unique; they intercede for us in Heaven for our holiness. When we pray to a Saint, they are interceding for us in their unique relationship with God, with their unique gifts of holiness. It is good to remember that it is always God who answers our prayers sent through a Saint.

Sitting down as a family, ponder the unique gifts of the Spirit God has given each family member. Have each "Saint in the making" draw out a picture of themselves as a Saint. Include in your picture the symbols of your Sainthood. For example, Carlo is pictured with technology, the Eucharist and a Rosary. What would you be a Patron Saint of? Carlo is quite often referred to as the Patron Saint of the Internet. Consider what others would pray to God for intercession to you, interceding for them in your unique relationship with God. Write down your inspirations and share them with each other. Commit, as a family, to daily encourage and pray for each other as you journey together to Sainthood.

You shall be holy to me, for I the Lord am holy, and have separated you from the peoples, that you should be mine. Leviticus 20:26

OUR LADY OF FATIMA

"Carlo used to say that it is very important to help the Virgin Mary accompany people in entrusting themselves to her Immaculate Heart, 'a safe port for all the ship-wrecks of this world,' as Sister Lucia defined it."
– Antonia, My Son Carlo

Sister Lucia was one of the three shepherd children that Our Lady of Fatima first appeared to on May 13th, 1917 in Fatima, Portugal. Lucia was 10 years old at the time of the apparitions. The apparitions and messages, along with those that followed in later years, are fully approved by the Catholic Church. Lucia describes the appearance of the Lady, "A lady dressed all in white, more brilliant than the sun, shedding rays of light, clear and stronger than a crystal glass filled with the most sparkling water, pierced by the burning rays of sun."

The Immaculate Heart of Our Lady of Fatima was radiating out, pouring into the three shepherd children the pure, sparkling love and the brilliant rays of light of our Lord and Savior, Jesus Christ, her Son. He is the eternal sun. She was radiating his glory, his light, his love for his children to learn to love as he loves through her pure Immaculate Heart.

She would ask the three children to return for six consecutive months. They returned. She continued to radiate God's light, enlightening them on his plan and will for their lives, to make them Saints.

In these divine appointments, she was giving them graces, inviting them to receive them and drawing the children into Her Heart to share a relationship

with her, a beautiful relationship as their mother, the Mother of God. She desired to teach them how to have an intimate relationship with her, with her Son, by consecrating themselves to her Immaculate Heart of pure love.

Jacinta, the youngest of the three shepherd children at age 7, desired to share a revelation from Our Lady before her death saying, "Tell everybody that God gives graces through the Immaculate Heart of Mary. Tell them to ask for graces from her, and that the Heart of Jesus wishes to be venerated with the Immaculate Heart of Mary."

The language of the heart is love. Our Lady is speaking to all of her children, all of humanity; with the simple gift of Her Heart and graces, God desires to give each soul through it.

At the Beatification ceremony of Jacinta, Pope St. John Paul II said, "I tell you that 'one makes more progress in a short time of submission and dependence in Mary than during entire years of personal initiatives, relying on oneself alone' (St. Louis de Montfort, The True devotion to the Blessed Virgin Mary, n.155) This was how the little shepherds became Saints so quickly." (Homily of his Holiness Pope John Paul II Beatification of Francesco and Jacinta Marto shepherds of Fatima).

Will you respond to her and accept the safe port of Her Immaculate Heart as Carlo did and become a Saint?

FAMILY ACTIVITY

Jesus is the Son of God. He is God. His rays of light, of love, his gifts of the Spirit to make us holy, pour out like the sun, radiating its rays over all of humanity. The three shepherd children observed Jesus' rays, more brilliant than the sun, filtering through his Mother, Our Lady of Fatima, radiating onto them to become Saints.

Have each family member place a clear glass, filled with water, directly in the sun. Observe the sparkling rays of light radiating out from the glasses from the sun. Draw and cut out Immaculate Hearts. Embellish the hearts, decorating Mary's Heart with your love for her and Jesus. On each Heart, write asking for the graces you would like to receive from Jesus and Mary, to grow in holiness. Place the hearts on the glasses. Pray asking Jesus to send his light, his love, his gifts of grace through the Immaculate Heart of Mary, to make your family a family of Saints.

Again Jesus spoke to them, saying, 'I am the light of the world; he who follows me will not walk in darkness, but will have the light of life.' John 8:12

1ST SATURDAY | WEEK 3

JESUS THROUGH MARY

"The heart of Jesus and the heart of Mary are indissolubly linked."
— Saint Carlo Acutis

Each child is a pure gift of love from God the Father. Our hearts are forever touched by this gift, this blessing, of pure joy. Families are forever changed, growing in love that expands beyond what they could have ever dreamed possible with the addition of each beloved child. Gazing, at the face of your child for the first time, is a moment that cannot be described. The delight you hold in your heart cannot be contained but radiates throughout your entire being.

Imagine Mary and Joseph looking at the face of the newborn baby Jesus for the first time. A child that was born of Mary, of her flesh, the divine face of God. Divinity and humanity indissolubly linked for eternity! The delight and joy for Mary and Joseph must have been indescribable. Imagine Jesus laying in the manger. Did rays of light emanate from his sweet Face? Did the glory of God surround him as it did for the shepherds in the field when the angels announced his birth? Did Mary and Joseph's hearts melt in overwhelming love and sing praises of thanksgiving when they looked at him?

The immense delight and unspeakable joy of God the Father could not be contained as he looked down from Heaven at his newborn Son. Divinity and humanity are united as one, his perfect gift to humanity, to the whole world, for their salvation. Only the

angels, singing in glory at the entrance of the Divine Child into this world, could welcome and proclaim the greatness of such a gift.

Saint Carlo Acutis said, "The biggest gift God gave to men was to send his only Son, Jesus Christ." Life is a pure gift. Mary chose to cooperate with God's plan, his will, and gave humanity the gift of the life of her newborn Son with her first fiat of "yes," becoming the Mother of God. She chose to give her second fiat of "yes", as a gift from her heart, at the foot of the cross. Together, Mother and Son, united as one heart, gave us to God the Father as Jesus died on the cross. The hearts of Jesus and Mary were an altar of love, offering themselves and us, in perfect obedience, in perfect love, a perfect gift.

We can choose to make our hearts a perfect gift to God, joining the hearts of Jesus and Mary in their offering. The Immaculate Heart of Mary always brings us to Jesus, who offers us as a gift to God the Father, in his sacrifice on the cross, as he died giving his life for us. The Blessed Mother desires that you receive the gift of her Immaculate Heart and the Sacred Heart of Jesus, as Carlo did. We can choose to receive their gift, to make our hearts a gift of love, joining their Hearts on the altar of their love for God. Being one with their hearts, with their love, will make us holy, will make us Saints.

A gift needs to be unwrapped, if it is to be received and enjoyed. How will you give your fiat of "yes" and unwrap this gift in your families, receiving the gift of holiness, of Sainthood, of perfect love?

TOGETHER WE PRAY . . .

Lord, we pray that our hearts may be indissolubly linked with Jesus' and Mary's Hearts. We ask that they may help us unwrap your gifts of holiness in our lives, in the Domestic Church of our family. We thank you for answering our prayer to be holy, to love as you love. In Jesus' name we pray. Amen

FAMILY ACTIVITY

God gave each of us the gift of life. "For you formed my inward parts, you knitted me together in my mother's womb. I praise you, for I am wondrously made. Wonderful are your works!" Psalm 139: 13-14. God's heart melts in love for each of us as our Heavenly Father! We are wondrously made, his royal sons and daughters. Each of our births hold a special place in the Heart of God. Our hearts, loving as he loves, are a gift to him. He desires that we unwrap his gifts of love that he sends all his children through the Hearts of Jesus and Mary, to be holy, Saints in the making.

Please find, if possible, a newborn or baby photo of each family member. Write down what you felt the moment you beheld the face of your child. Wrap both as a gift for each child to unwrap. Unwrap them, talking about your delight in each birth, your love for each child. Imagine together the overwhelming delight God had at the moment he beheld the Face of Jesus at his birth. Think about God's delight when he first beheld the face of each child, including your own, born into His Family! Unwrap God's love for your family, receiving his gift of holiness, his overwhelming love as his children.

For God so loved the world that he gave his only-begotten Son, that whoever believes in him should not perish but have eternal life. John 3:16

BAPTISM

"He told me that our time on earth was not enough to thank Jesus for having given us Baptism, and that so many people do not realize what an infinite gift it is to receive it."
Antonia, "My Son Carlo"

Carlo was born in London on May 3rd, 1991. Fifteen days after his birth, on May 18th, his parents brought him to Our Lady of Dolours Church in Chelsea, London. It was at this Church, dedicated to Our Lady of Fatima, that he received the Sacrament of Baptism. Thus, he was dedicated to her Immaculate Heart. In this most momentous of days, Carlo received the gift from Jesus of becoming a child of God, baptized by the cleansing water, the fire of love-the Holy Spirit.

St. Maximillian Kolbe remarked about the significance of the Sacrament of Baptism, "The soul is regenerated in the sacred waters of Baptism and thus becomes God's child." This special day of his Baptism, Carlo, was born into the Heavenly family of God the Father. This day is extra special as it is shared by the birth of another amazing Saint. Pope St. John Paul II was born into this world on May 18th, 1920. He and Carlo both shared a deep devotion to Mary's Immaculate Heart, entrusting themselves fully to her maternal care as their Heavenly Mother.

Saint Carlo Acutis proclaimed that, "The Virgin Mother is the only woman in my life." At the very beginning, Pope St. John Paul II dedicated his pontificate to Jesus through Mary, choosing the Latin motto, "Totus Tuus," totally yours. In his book, "Gift and Mystery," Pope St. John Paul II described this beautiful entrustment to Mary's maternal charity, her Immaculate Heart. Here she, "cares for the brethren of her Son...in whose birth and development she cooperates," through the gift of the Spirit of Jesus, her Son, a gift we were all given at our Baptisms.

Both Carlo and Pope St. John Paul II lived this gift of Baptism daily, of total entrustment to the Blessed Mother; which was influenced by the teachings of St. Louis de Montfort. He wrote, "True Devotion to Mary." St. Louis de Montfort believed that, "Mary has produced, together with the Holy Ghost, the greatest thing which has ever been or ever will be - a God-man; and she will consequently produce the greatest Saints that there will be in the end of time."

Mary gave birth to Jesus, the God-man. Through the love and action of the Holy Spirit she became the Mother of God. She bore Jesus into this world; Divinity breaking into humanity. She raised him, with the help of St. Joseph, to be whom he was meant to be, our Redeemer and Savior. Jesus has given, to all who are Baptized, the gift of Mary as our Mother. We are all her children. With her pure, Immaculate Heart, Mary loves us more than we can begin to contemplate as she loves as God loves. She desires to give the gift to love God and to learn to love as he loves through her Immaculate Heart, becoming who we are meant to be, the greatest of Saints.

Jesus desires to share his Mother with our families, with each of his children, taking her Immaculate Heart into theirs. Will you thank Jesus for his gift of Baptism, receiving the gift of the Immaculate Heart of his Mother, to form you and your family into the greatest of Saints?

TOGETHER WE PRAY . . .

Lord, we thank you for the gift of Baptism, being born into your Heavenly family as your child. We thank you for the gift of the Holy Family, Jesus, Mary and Joseph, for their example of love. We pray, asking for their intercession, for our family to be formed into the greatest of Saints. We ask for our family's holiness, to love as you love, in the name of Jesus. Amen

FAMILY ACTIVITY

At our Baptism, we are all given the gift of royalty, sons and daughters of God the Father! We receive the beautiful gift to be part of the royal, Holy Family of Jesus, Mary and Joseph. They are all our Heavenly family, forming us to be the greatest of Saints, as we participate in one Holy Family of Love.

If possible, find a picture of each family member's Baptism. Make a copy, writing on the copy the date of the Baptism. Position the copies of the pictures in a prominent place in your home. These are your family's heavenly birthdays!!

THROW A ROYAL, HEAVENLY BIRTHDAY PARTY!!

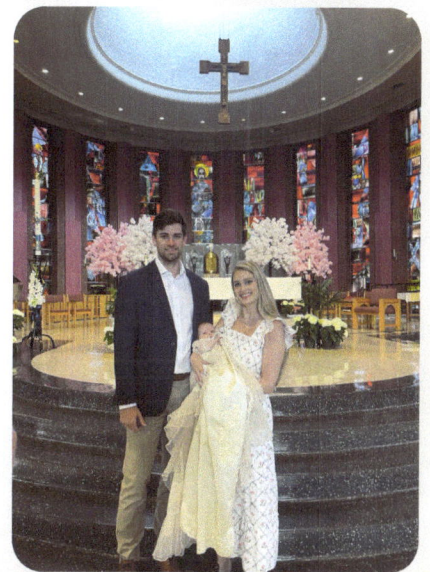

...one Lord, one faith, one baptism, one God and Father of us all, who is above all and through all and in all. Ephesians 4:4–6

OUR LADY OF MOUNT CARMEL

"I remember how, when he (Carlo) was four, I gave him a gold chain with a medal with the scapular of the Virgin Mary of Mount Carmel. It had been given to me by one of my great-grandmothers on the day of my Baptism. From that moment on, he never took it off, and he told me, 'This way I will always have Jesus and the Virgin Mary close to my heart.'" Antonia, My Son Carlo

At the apparition of July 13th, 1917, Our Lady of Fatima had promised the children, if they returned on October 13th, she would perform a miracle that all in attendance could see and believe. Our Lady would not disappoint them. Over the course of the prior months, after Our Lady's first appearance, more and more people had been joining the children on the appointed days. Returning on October 13th, the children were joined by an estimated crowd of over 70,000 people. In attendance were believers as well as skeptics. Fulfilling the earlier promise of Our Lady to the children, reporters and photographers would officially proclaim to the world, in print and in photographs, the "miracle of the sun."

In 1930, after an extensive investigation, the Catholic Church would officially recognize the events and miracle that took place at Fatima as "worthy of belief." During the miracle, it reportedly was seen up to 25 miles away. When all eyes were on the dancing sun, Lucia, Jacinta, and Francisco were receiving various visions, including mysteries of the rosary being played out before them. The children saw, in the third vision, Our Lady of Mount Carmel. In this glorious vision, she was crowned as Queen of Heaven and earth, holding the child Jesus near her heart. She held in her hands a brown scapular.
Our Lady of Mount Carmel appeared to St. Simon

Stock, on July 16th, 1251, giving him the brown scapular as a gift to the Carmelites from their Heavenly Mother. She gave him the promise that, "whosoever dies in this garment shall not suffer eternal fire." Wearing the brown scapular is a devotion of silent prayer to our Heavenly Mother. It's a gift to her of veneration, of confidence and of love. Eventually, extended to all the laity, the wearer of the brown scapular or the medal, after being blessed by a Priest, also receives the promises of Our Lady of Mount Carmel.

Sister Lucia, responding to a question about the connection between the scapular and the rosary said, "Yes, the rosary and the scapular are inseparable…Our Lady held in her hands the scapular because she wants us all to wear it. The scapular is a sign of our consecration to Our Lady. All Catholics should wear the scapular as part of the Fatima message."

Pope St. John Paul II was a big proponent of Catholics wearing the brown scapular. He declared publicly in 2002 that, "I too have worn the scapular of Carmel over my heart for a long time." Carlo's mother described the scapular as, "one of the devotions to which my son was especially attached…he had one of the Carmelite priests bless it when he was seven years old. He alternated the cloth scapular with the gold one that he had been given."

Pope St. John Paul II and Carlo desired to keep Jesus and Mary close to their hearts, to love her as their Heavenly Mother as Jesus asked of them. Carlo declared, "To always be close to Jesus, that's my life's plan." The closer we are to Jesus and Mary here on earth, the closer we will be to them in heaven. What is your family's plan to be as close to Jesus and Mary as you can?

TOGETHER WE PRAY . . .

Lord, we desire to be as close to Jesus and Mary as we possibly can, here on earth and in Heaven. Help us to make this our life plan and act on it. Please draw us close to you in love as your children; closer than we could ever imagine to be, for all of eternity. In the name of Jesus we pray. Amen

FAMILY ACTIVITY

Draw closer in understanding of the miraculous events of Fatima as a family. Be drawn into the lives of the three shepherd children in an unique film experience. Engage the whole family in an old-fashioned movie night! Watch the original 1952 film by Warner Brothers, "The Miracle of Our Lady of Fatima - Blessed Virgin Mary Apparition," on the Catholic Worldwide YouTube channel.

Please take care to preview the section of the film where the three shepherd children receive a vision of hell, skipping this section, if needed, for younger children. This film was shot on location in Portugal, only 35 years after the Apparitions and "miracle of the sun" took place. It received an Oscar-Nomination for its score. The film is cited as being reverent, sincere and faithful to the events, evoking a sense of spirituality and hope. Enjoy a film experience from yesteryear with your family and bring out the popcorn!

Draw near to God and he will draw near to you...

James 4:8

LOVE GOD WITH ALL YOUR HEART

"My son was convinced that the beauty of life does not depend on its length but rather whether we are able to make God the most important part of it. He believed that was what made a successful life. He said that 'loving God above all else' should be the ideal goal for everyone's life. Carlo believed that if we were able to achieve this high objective, we would receive the keys to open the gates that lead to Heaven directly from God." –Antonia, "My Son Carlo"

Carlo would not live a long life. He died of a rare form of Leukemia at the age of 15 on October 12th, 2006. He did live, however, a full life, a beautiful life, a successful life, according to his definition. His life was filled with love for God, with love for his neighbor. He achieved his goal, his high objective. He was given the keys directly from the hand of Jesus, his "good Friend," and walked through the open gates into heaven, becoming a Saint. He was meant to be a Saint. We are all meant to be Saints.

Carlo became a Saint living a typical, normal childhood. His parents were wealthy and well positioned in Italian society. Many around Carlo were unaware of these temporal advantages. He was very simple and unassuming. Wealth and position were not his treasure. Yet in his presence, there was something very special about him that radiated out to others. Recalling his interactions with Carlo, a parish priest familiar with him, shared these words with his mother after his death, "All these memories have something in common, something striking: the perception that Carlo had an absolutely normal way of living but an absolutely special kind of harmony." "My Son Carlo"

This harmony was his deep love, with all his heart, for God. Carlo made God the most important part of his life. He integrated this love and close relationship with God in every moment of his life. His mother shared in her book, "It was natural for him to interrupt his daily activities to pray. His relationship with God was continuous, incessant. Everything he did, he thought of God, turning to him. His prayers helped him, as he's said, to gather up energy and start the day's activities with increased strength and serenity."

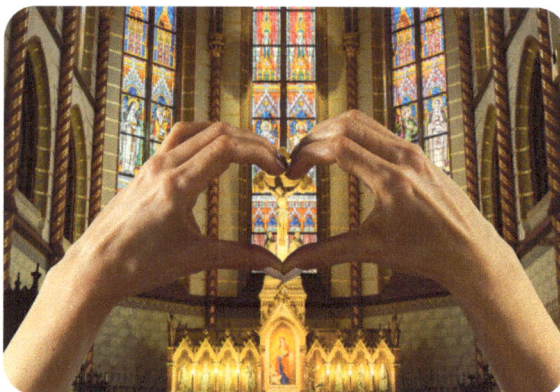

You always give your best to what you love. Carlo gave God his best. He treasured God above all things, giving him all of his heart, all of his life. St. Leo the Great describes the treasure Carlo had found: "The good and chaste soul is so happy to be filled with God that it desires to take delight in nothing else…where delight and enjoyment are found, there the heart's desire is attached."

Carlo took delight and enjoyment in his relationship with God, being filled with God. It was his heart's desire to live in a chaste, pure, respectful relationship with God and with all those around him. St. Barnabas, Apostle, is credited with saying in 61 AD, "For your souls good make every effort to love chastely." Carlo made every effort he could. He achieved his heart's desire. In his sainthood he is recognized for his purity. He loved God with all his heart. He encouraged others around him to love chastely with purity, with respectfulness, regardless of their station in life; giving their best to God and treasuring him with all their hearts.

Making his heart an altar of chaste, pure love to God, Carlo lived a beautiful, full life. He drew close to God, making him the most important part of his life. As the Mother of God, Mary, is the one who is closest to God. Jesus was her whole life. She loves him with the altar of her pure Immaculate Heart. She desires to help us draw close to him, making our hearts an altar to love God. Will you accept her Immaculate Heart and live a beautiful, full life treasuring God with all of your heart as Carlo did?

TOGETHER WE PRAY...

Hear, O Israel: The Lord our God is one Lord, and you shall love the Lord your God with all your heart, and with all your soul, and with all your might. And these words which I command you this day shall be upon your heart; and you shall teach them diligently to your children, and shall talk of them when you sit in your house, and when you walk by the way, and when you lie down, and when you rise. And you shall bind them as a sign upon your hand, and they shall be as frontlets between your eyes. And you shall write them on the doorposts of your house and on your gates.

Deuteronomy 6:4–9

FAMILY ACTIVITY

Carlo loved God with all his heart, his heart was an altar of love. God was his heart's desire, treasuring him above all things. Carlo delighted in his continuous relationship with God. He would interrupt his day to pray for guidance, to be in harmony, in union with God in love, setting goals and objectives that he achieved with the help of daily prayer.

The first Domestic Church was in the home of Jesus, Mary and Joseph, the Holy Family. Choose a spot in your Domestic Church, constructing an altar of love for God, a quiet place of prayer to treasure God. God's children are the treasures of His Heart. Treasure His Heart. Have each family member write or draw a love letter to Him, placing them on the altar; thanking Him for his love and care for your holy family.

CHARITY

"Everything passes away....the only thing that will make us truly beautiful in God's eyes is the way that we have loved him and our brothers."

—Saint Carlo Acutis

Going beyond loving God with all his heart, Carlo was called by Jesus, as we all are called, to love his neighbor as himself. There was no distinction for him. He served the poor who were in need of material and spiritual wealth. Antonia has said that, "Every person was important to Carlo....in each one he saw the face of Jesus." Carlo lived to love God, loving his neighbor, all of his neighbors, in beautiful charity. "My Son Carlo"

Carlo placed others above himself, living each moment in charity. He saw what was needed and attended to those needs. Carlo was known to buy, with his own money, sleeping bags and fill thermos with hot food for the homeless of Milan. He turned down more clothing or new shoes so he could use the money to help someone who needed it more than he did. As a child, he brought to school his piggy bank, giving it to another child who was in need. He volunteered at soup kitchens, giving his savings, enabling 2,500 meals to be given to the poor in Milan.

Carlo gave to others using his God given "gift" of phenomenal computer skills to help parishes, tutor and build websites. His tender heart stood up and defended those who were bullied or disabled. He taught catechumens how to love God and to become Saints with his "holiness kit." He spent time in prayer and offered up little sacrifices for the needs of others. He was a "light" for his many friends, spending time helping them during hardships. As an example for them, he stood firm in defense of purity in relationships and in his belief that abortion was wrong. He would tell them, "Act like me and you will see the results." The results were a beautiful full life, a life of a Saint, lived in charity. St. John of the Cross said, "At the end of our life, we shall all be judged by charity." Carlo wanted to be judged on his actions of charity, not of the things of this world. Antonia described Carlo's life of charity, "In fact, he worries little about himself. Each day he was dedicated to others, to his world, which was in the end small but in his heart special and unique…but he did not do anything extraordinary - just ordinary things with a lot of heart, "My Son Carlo". Carlo's heart was filled with the self-giving love of God, with Jesus. Acting on this love, he lived his ordinary existence extraordinarily. This love, exemplified in the life of Carlo, was the invisible fire of the Holy Spirit.

The fire of God's love, his Spirit, had come down in visible form at Pentecost, filling the Blessed Mother and the disciples. Following Pentecost, the ordinary disciples went out to all the world in charity. They proclaimed the salvation of God extraordinarily. The Blessed Mother was filled with the Holy Spirit from her conception. She was always filled with extraordinary grace, with extraordinary charity. She observed all around her, attending to everything with the fire of the love of God. At the wedding in Cana, it was she who saw the need for more wine. It was she who told the servants to do all that her Son asked. From the beginning of the formation of the Catholic Church, it was Mary, the Tabernacle of the Son of God, who guided the disciples. It is she who sees all that we need to become Saints. Within the refuge of her Immaculate Heart, we will be formed into Saints by the fire of the Holy Spirit, beautiful in God's eyes.

As sons and daughters, the fire of God's love perfects all in his love, by his love, for his love, to love and be loved for all of eternity in a beautiful, Holy Family of love. Taking refuge in her Immaculate heart, Carlo lived a life of charity as God's son, beautiful in his eyes. How will your family take refuge in the Immaculate Heart of Mary as Carlo did, beautiful in charity as sons and daughters perfected in love, Saints in the making?

TOGETHER WE PRAY . . .

Lord, help us to see the needs of all those around us, that in acting on those needs, we may be beautiful in your eyes in charity. Thank you for all of the blessings we have received from your bountiful hands. In the name of Jesus we pray. Amen

FAMILY ACTIVITY

In the apparitions of Our Lady of Fatima, she requested the children to, "Pray, pray a lot, and offer sacrifices for sinners." Carlo's mother shares that Carlo obeyed the request of Our Lady of Fatima's, "words to the letter and always felt guilty because he did not make enough sacrifices and pray enough for those who were far from God," "My Son Carlo."

As a family, pray asking God for ideas about how you can offer up sacrifices this week for each other and for those in need. Place the ideas in a box. Praying to the Holy Spirit, have each family member draw out a sacrifice. Know that no sacrifice, in the eyes of God, is too small if it comes from the heart in self-giving love. Our Lady of Fatima encouraged the children in their prayers and sacrifices, promising, "Don't be discouraged. I shall never abandon you. My Immaculate Heart will be your refuge and, through it, will conduct you to God." She gives us all this promise!

He who has a bountiful eye will be blessed, for he shares his bread with the poor Proverbs 22:9

EUCHARIST

"The Eucharist is my highway to Heaven." —Saint Carlo Acutis

Carlo received the Body, Blood, Soul and Divinity of Jesus at seven, which was early for an Italian youth. He had asked to receive First Holy Communion early; being well prepared by the Holy Spirit to receive Jesus in the fullness of faith, given by grace. Carlo fully believed in his heart, that hidden in the consecrated host was the true Body of Jesus and the consecrated wine was the true Blood of Jesus. He would simply state his profound belief of Jesus' Real Presence in the Eucharist, "my highway to Heaven-The Eucharist is truly the heart of Jesus."

Receiving the very heart of Jesus in the Eucharist, Carlo would say, "Jesus, come right in, make yourself at home!" Jesus answered the prayer of Carlo's heart with his own heart's desire, "...If a man loves me, he will keep my word, and my father will love him, and we will come to him and make our home with him," (John 14:23). Jesus confirmed Carlo's profound belief of Jesus' heart in the Eucharist with a promise before his ascension into heaven, "...I am with you always, to the close of the age," (Matthew 28:20). Jesus keeps his promise to stay with us. He is really, truly, substantially present in the Eucharist.

Carlo knew that he was eating and drinking the Body and Blood of Jesus in every Eucharist, at every Catholic Mass, in every Catholic Church. He declared, "Through the Eucharist, we are transformed into love." Jesus is the Eucharist. He gives himself to us to eat as our spiritual food. Love desires to act, to give of itself. Jesus is the very essence of transforming love, perfect love in action. He desires all of his children to be holy, to be Saints. His cross is love perfectly revealed in action, "Greater love has no man than this, that a man lay down his life for his friends," (John 15:13). Carlo

relied on the action of love, the transforming power of the fire of the cross of Jesus, his "good Friend," in the Eucharist. Carlo built an intimate relationship with Jesus, living a fully Eucharistic life, that transformed him into a Saint by receiving the Body, Blood, Soul and Divinity of Jesus in the Eucharist. He fully believed in Jesus' Real Presence in the consecrated bread and wine.

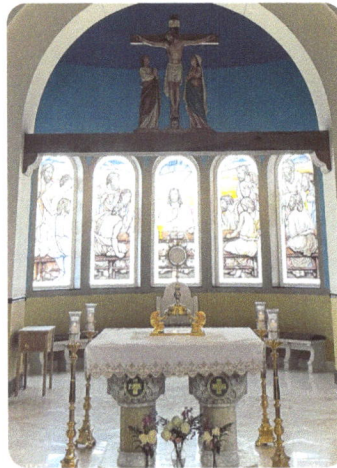

His mother testifies to the effect of the Eucharist on Carlo, "With the help of the Eucharist, his life was transformed into a highway to Heaven, as he liked to define it. Another highway to heaven is the grace that he continues to spread to those who pray to him," "My Son Carlo". Carlo loved Jesus with all his heart. He wanted to spread this love he had for Jesus in the Eucharist. Through the action of grace, the fire of the love of the Holy Spirit, Carlo acted by becoming God's influencer for the Eucharist.

Carlo could not understand that sports stadiums and concerts were full of people, but churches containing the Real Presence of Jesus were empty. He determined, "They have to see, they have to understand." Acting on his desire for others to know the truth of the Eucharist, at the age of eleven, Carlo started creating a website about the Vatican approved Eucharistic Miracles of the World. He finished the website one year before his death. Using the most current advances in technology, many of the most recent miracles have been scientifically tested. The results reveal what Carlo already knew in his heart through faith. The consecrated host IS the suffering Heart of Jesus. Carlo's highway to Heaven, the Eucharist, truly is the Sacred Heart of Jesus!

"The more we receive the Eucharist, the more we will become like Jesus, so that on this earth we will have a foretaste of Heaven." Saint Carlo Acutis. We are what we eat. Carlo lived a life focused on receiving Jesus in the Eucharist. Will you pray and ask Carlo for grace to live a fully Eucharistic centered life? Will your family make the Eucharist your "highway to Heaven;" receiving Jesus' Body, Blood, Soul and Divinity, becoming more like Jesus, becoming Saints?

TOGETHER WE PRAY . . .

O God make me a productive grain, efficient grain, effective grain. Jesus, make me a grain of wheat so that I can reach your Eucharistic reality, by which I really and truly live. - Prayer of Saint Carlo Acutis

FAMILY ACTIVITY

God answered Carlo's prayer; making him a very productive grain. Carlo's website of Vatican approved Eucharistic Miracles of the World and his International Exhibit of Eucharistic Miracle panels have made a tremendous impact all over the world, sowing seeds for eternal life! Carlo was particularly interested in the miracle of Lanciano, Italy of 750 A.D. He visited the miracle on display many times, using it to evangelize the truth of the Real Presence of Jesus in the Eucharist.

Visit Carlo's website, www.miracolieucaristici.org. As a family, read about the Lanciano, Italy Eucharistic Miracle. For younger children, act out Rimini, the miracle of the mule involving St. Anthony of Padua. There are many other amazing Eucharistic Miracles on Carlo's website to read and learn about. Enjoy learning of God's goodness, mercy and love for us, truly present in the Eucharist.

So Jesus said to them, 'Truly, truly, I say to you, unless you eat the flesh of the Son of man and drink his blood, you have no life in you; he who eats my flesh and drinks my blood has eternal life, and I will raise him up at the last day. *John 6:53-54*

SCRIPTURE

"If we only knew what eternity is, we would do everything to change the course of our lives.....To love what awaits us tomorrow is to give today the best of our fruit." – Saint Carlo Acutis

Carlo desired to love God as he loves, with his whole heart, within the Immaculate Heart of Mary, giving God the best of his fruit, all of himself. He didn't wait to change the course of his life. Daily, looking forward to Heaven, he lived and loved in the moment, looking at eternity.

To truly, authentically love something, in order to daily give yourself totally over to what you love, you need to know what you love. In knowing, you may truly, and authentically give yourself over to it. Carlo sought to know God daily, to love God for who God is, to change the course of his life, to be a Saint. He desired an intimate, loving relationship built on righteousness. A right relationship with God is holiness brought by knowing and loving God as God loves. Fourth century Doctor of the Catholic Church and translator of the Vulgate, St. Jerome said, "Ignorance of the Scripture is ignorance of Christ." Carlo knew Christ and the Scriptures, immersing himself in both daily.

Carlo, believing that the gospels were a gift from God, loved to immerse himself in them to learn to be more like Jesus. "If you believe what you like in the gospels, and reject what you don't like, it's not the gospels you believe, but yourself," St. Augustine. Carlo wanted to know the truth of God, the truth of what awaited him for eternity. Believing in God's truth, not his own, he becomes like Jesus. Knowing and loving God, he sought to be as close as he could to Jesus here on earth. The closer we mirror God's image here, the closer we will be to the Eternal Beatitude in eternity. Carlo desired with all his heart to be as close to God as he could in Heaven for eternity.

Drawing close to God requires work on our part; it requires our heart. "Draw near to God and he will draw near to you. Cleanse your hands, you sinners, and purify your hearts, you men of double mind." (James 4:8) Carlo was of one mind, putting in the required work. No matter what the cost, he cleansed and purified his heart with the help of the Immaculate Heart of Mary. He did what was needed to bring forth fruit here on earth, reaping the benefits of that fruit for eternity. St. John Chrysostom advised that, "The Holy Scriptures were not given to us that we should enclose them in books, but that we should engrave them upon our hearts." Carlo took this advice to heart, writing the written Word of God daily on his heart.

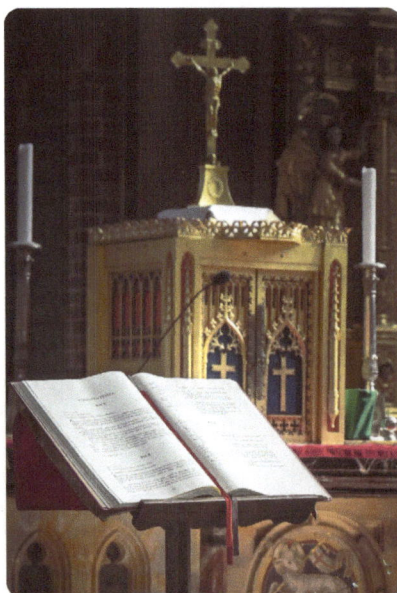

Receiving and experiencing the Sacred Heart of Jesus daily in the Eucharist; he desired to know the heart of God in the Scriptures to love him more fully. Describing Carlo's daily immersion into Scripture his mother said, "Everyday, he concentrated on a small passage which became his compass he used to guide his day." "My Son Carlo" Carlo used the Bible daily as his compass to know God and change his life, to become holy- to be a Saint. Carlo said, "Holiness is not the process of adding, but subtracting: less of me to leave space for God." Daily he was cleansing and purifying his heart with Scripture. Carlo, with the Immaculate Heart of Mary, was making room for God to change him into the image of Jesus with the reception of the Eucharist, the Sacred Heart of Jesus.

Where our treasure is, there is our heart. Carlo's heart treasured God's heart, experiencing him in the Eucharist and in Scripture. Pope St. Gregory the Great exclaimed, "Learn the heart of God from the Word of God." Carlo was learning and taking Jesus into his heart, daily changing into a Saint. Will you join Carlo, using the Bible as your daily compass, becoming a Saint? Will your family, with the help of the Immaculate Heart of Mary, work to change into the image of Jesus, drawing closer to him and the Eternal Beatitude of Heaven?

TOGETHER WE PRAY . . .

Lord, we desire to give you the best of our fruit today by knowing you truly for who you are. Help us to know you, loving you with all our hearts. Draw us closer to you in love, changing our lives, preparing us for eternity with you in Heaven. In Jesus' name we pray. Amen

FAMILY ACTIVITY

The Eucharist is a person. It is Jesus Christ, his Sacred Heart present for all of us in the Sacrament of his love. Carlo read Scripture daily to know God, making room in his heart to draw closer to God. Carlo, working with his heart in love, prepared for eternity.

Prepare your family, their hearts, for eternity by reading the Scriptures with them. Read the Bread of Life Discourse, John chapter six, with your family. Discuss Jesus' interaction with the Jews, with his disciples and the truth of his words in light of the Lanciano, Italy Eucharistic Miracle. For younger children act out the Biblical story involving another amazing animal, a donkey, and an angel in Numbers 22. Make room in your family's hearts, receiving the treasures stored up for them in Heaven.

...but lay up for yourselves treasures in heaven, where neither moth nor rust consumes and where thieves do not break in and steal. For where your treasure is, there will your heart be also. Matthew 6:20-21

ATTEND MASS WEEKLY

"You go straight to Heaven if you participate in the Mass every day!" *— Saint Carlo Acutis*

Carlo began to attend Mass daily after taking his first Holy Communion at seven years old. Even at this young age, he understood in his heart the need to receive the Eucharist as often as was possible. He strove to grow in holiness, to be in daily union with Jesus. Daily he was set on fire with love for God, to love as God loves, becoming a Saint. God had placed the flame of love for the Holy Eucharist in Carlo's heart with his very first union with the Body and Blood of Jesus. Helping build his union with Jesus, those around him, fanned the flame of love of the Holy Spirit, making the commitment to bring him to daily Mass - to "go straight to Heaven."

Antonia shares from his First Holy Communion: "Certainly, union with the Eucharistic Jesus was at the heart of Carlo's day from that moment onward. Starting on that day, he went to Mass everyday. His relationship with the Body of Christ had become 'LIFE.'...During Mass, he conversed with him, he spoke to him, he listened to his words, and he took inspiration and energy from his actions. His creativity and constructive energy flowed outward from his daily Mass attendance," "My Son Carlo." Carlo lived a fully Eucharistic life by daily attending Mass, forming an intimate relationship with Jesus. He made the daily reception of the Eucharist, the Body, Blood, Soul and Divinity of Jesus, the center of his life. Just as Mary had made Jesus the center of her life, Carlo took refuge within the Immaculate Heart of Mary - to "go straight to Heaven" as Mary did at her Assumption.

Carlo did not just "attend" Mass and check it off as fulfilling his weekly obligation. He actively participated in Mass, paying attention to what was taking place. He was present, in each moment, to the workings of the Holy Spirit, the fire of God's love, within himself. Carlo responded to the inspirations of Jesus during the Mass, incorporating them throughout his day. With docility from the Holy Spirit, he eagerly opened his heart to the teaching of the Liturgy of the Word, the Holy Scriptures. He experienced the Body and Blood of Jesus during the Liturgy of the Eucharist, filling his heart with the fire of the cross - with the Sacred Heart of Jesus.

Carlo's persistent attendance at Mass resulted in an intimate friendship with Jesus as his "good Friend." Describing his friendship Carlo said, "The Lord is the only person that we don't have to ask if he's available. I can always confide something in him. I can also complain or question him in silent moments and tell him the things that I don't understand. Then I find within me some words he sends me; some passages from the Gospel that cloaks me in security and confidence." Jesus responded to Carlo's daily reliance on him and persistent pursuit of his friendship. With a Word, a passage of Scripture, Jesus' constant presence as Carlo's "good Friend" made Carlo feel secure and confident in his arms of love, the fire of Jesus' Cross.

Jesus' arms of love, with the Immaculate Heart of Mary, are constantly open, waiting for us to pursue his friendship, especially during Mass. Antonia shared, "At Mass, Jesus offers himself to the Father because of his love for us. Carlo used to say that if we were to realize the infinite value of every single Mass for eternal life, churches would be full to the brim," "My Son Carlo." With the Immaculate Heart of Mary, will you pray to Carlo for the grace to fully participate at weekly Mass, realizing its infinite value for eternity?

TOGETHER WE PRAY . . .

Lord, we come to you asking to go straight to Heaven, in union with Jesus, through our participation at Mass and reception of the Holy Eucharist. We pray for the Holy Spirit to fan the flame of love in us for Jesus, your son, that we may grow in holiness, in an intimate loving friendship with him as our good friend. Thank you for answering our prayers. In Jesus' name we pray. Amen

FAMILY ACTIVITY

Actively participating at Mass and consuming the Holy Eucharist, Carlo, built an intimate relationship with Jesus as the center of his life. He relied on the presence of Jesus who is always with us! Carlo knew the value of every Mass, where Jesus is offering himself, his very life, as a sacrifice to God the Father for us to have eternal life with him in Heaven.

View "The Veil Removed," a beautiful, short 5 ½ minute film on the Mass, with your family. Watch on their website at: theveilremoved.com. They describe their film as revealing:…"the coming together of heaven and earth at Mass, as seen by saints and mystics, revealed by Scripture and in the catechism of the Catholic Church." Earth, respond to Jesus, let him lift your veil in the Mass, open your hearts to receive your Savior and King, giving him praise and honor for his sacrifice for you.

Let us hold fast the confession of our hope without wavering, for he who promised is faithful; and let us consider how to stir up one another to love and good works, not neglecting to meet together, as is the habit of some, but encouraging one another, and all the more as you see the Day drawing near. Hebrews 10:23-25

VISIT JESUS IN THE TABERNACLE

"If we reflected on this seriously, we would never leave him alone in the tabernacles waiting for us with love, wanting to help us and to support us on our earthly journey." — Saint Carlo Acutis

On reflection, we realize that the first tabernacle Jesus took up residence in, out of love, was that of his mother. Giving him her heart in love, Mary first conceived Jesus in the tabernacle of her holy Immaculate Heart. She then conceived Jesus, through the Holy Spirit, in the tabernacle of her womb, giving him her flesh in love as his mother. Mary is the Immaculate Conception, as told to St. Bernadette. She was full of grace through the gift of love of the Holy Spirit. She was completely holy, loving as God loves, from the moment of her conception. Only the flesh of Mary's body, her Immaculate Womb, was worthy to be the tabernacle for the Son of God the Father. She gave her Son, Jesus Christ, the humanity of her flesh. As mother and child, they are one in union of flesh and heart.

The essence of pure Love takes the form of a child in our humanity. Divinity breaks into humanity, blessing all flesh. At Mary's "Fiat" of yes, the Holy Spirit works intimately within Mary. She becomes the "living tabernacle" of the Son of God the Father. The Holy Trinity is dynamically acting in love for all of humanity through Mary. Saint Carlo Acutis said, "The tabernacle is a synonym for a cradle of grace. The most Holy Trinity operates in the Tabernacle. I see the tabernacle as dynamic. The Eucharistic reality is the proof and confirmation and verification of their destination of holiness." Cradling the Holy Divine child, first in her heart and womb before she cradled him in her arms, Mary tabernacled the Holy Eucharist as the Holy of Holies.

The cradle of Mary's arms and of her Immaculate Heart were always a refuge of love for Jesus. She helped and supported him throughout his mission, his earthly journey. Jesus works through Mary, in all of his sons and daughters, as mediatrix of all grace. She gives us grace, through the Holy Spirit, to help support us throughout our earthly journey, to make us holy as sons and daughters of God the Father. "Grace is given or regiven by the sacraments. The tabernacle is close to that which is holy. It is intimate with it. Spending time with that which is holy makes it holy, as well. So, visiting the tabernacle means making oneself a candidate for holiness," Saint Carlo Acutis. Mary, the living tabernacle of Jesus, is the one most intimate with her Son, who is the Holy Eucharist.

Jesus desires that we visit him in the tabernacle where he waits ready to make us holy, to be who we were meant to be - Saints. He desires that we draw close to the tabernacle of his Holy Mother, visiting her, taking her Immaculate Heart into ours. Mary waits for us to ask her to give us her Immaculate Heart to help us on our journey to Jesus, to the Trinity. She desires to tabernacle all of her sons and daughters within her Immaculate Heart, the holy of holies, with Jesus, making us Saints. The Holy of Holies was God's presence among his people. It was a place of profound awe and reverence. How will you and your family respond to the desires of Jesus and Mary in the presence of the tabernacles of majesty and holiness?

TOGETHER WE PRAY . . .

Lord, receive our prayer of thanksgiving for the Living Tabernacle of Mary, as our own Tabernacle of refuge. We thank you for the gift of grace and mercy, in the cradle of her loving arms, that we receive from your Holy Will for our journey to Heaven as your royal children. In Jesus' name we pray. Amen

FAMILY ACTIVITY

Mary is the Holy Mother of God the Son, Jesus Christ. Not waiting, respond, act in love and leap into her open arms of love. She is ready and waiting to hug her royal sons and daughters close to her heart.

Using a box, with flaps that open in the middle, construct a tabernacle; decorating it for the Immaculate Heart of Mary and the Sacred Heart of Jesus. Place the tabernacle on your home altar, keeping it there for the duration of your family's consecration journey. Write or draw love letters to Jesus and Mary. Place them in the tabernacle, in thanksgiving for the gifts of love and support on your earthly journey to Heaven, to be one Holy Family of Love.

Behind the second curtain stood a tent called the Holy of Holies, having the golden altar of incense and the ark of the covenant covered on all sides with gold, which contained a golden urn holding the manna, and Aaron's rod that budded, and the tables of the covenant; above it were the cherubim of glory overshadowing the mercy seat... Hebrews 9:3-5

IMMACULATE HEART OF MARY

"For Carlo, immersing himself in God through meditation and prayer was like entering into heaven through a secret door and sitting down in his place in eternity for a moment. Carlo had a contemplative spirit. He was always thinking of God, who became the guide of his heart and his actions.' — Antonia

As Carlo walked his short journey here on earth, he always had his eyes on eternity. Entering heaven on earth, through prayer and meditation, God became the heavenly guide of Carlo's heart and of his actions. Sitting down, right where he was placed, he did God's will. Present every moment to eternity, he loved God, his family, his friends and all of his neighbors with all his heart and in his actions.

Guided by God, in the midst of daily life, Carlo found a secret door to heaven. He was directed to this door of holiness, to become who he was meant to be - a Saint. We are all directed by God to this secret door of holiness, to love as he loves, to become Saints!

Accepting the key to the secret door, Carlo walked right through, becoming a Saint! The secret door to heaven is through the tabernacle of the Immaculate Heart of Mary. The key to this secret door is consecration to her Immaculate Heart. More is needed to become holy than just the acceptance of the key. We need to open the secret door of our hearts to grace, to accept her Heart, her love. Receiving the gift of Mary's Immaculate Heart into our hearts and accepting our Heavenly Mother into the domestic church of our home, she brings us grace to love her Son Jesus, to love as he loves.

Antonia, Carlo's mother, says, "He had read Pope St. John Paul II's encyclical 'Ecclesia de Eucharistia,' which urges all believers to place themselves 'at the school of Mary, a woman of the Eucharistia.' In fact, no one can better introduce us than Mary on how to worship her son [present] in each Eucharist for our salvation…" "My Son Carlo." We need to sit at the feet of our Mother, the Mother of God, and learn from her for our salvation. Devotion to the Immaculate Heart of Mary inspires us to contemplate and meditate on her virtues given by grace, especially those of forgiveness, mercy and selflessness. Cultivating her virtues, draws us into the selfless, self-giving love of Jesus, her Son, the Eucharist. We learn to love as he loves, a mirror of the love of God, Saints.

We are all Saints in the making. Jesus desires to work through his Mother for our heavenly salvation, to make us Saints through grace. He desires our devotion to her Immaculate Heart. During the visions of Fatima on June 13th, 1917, Lucia asked the Lady to bring them to Heaven. The Lady responded directly to Lucia saying, "Jesus wishes to use you in order to make me known and loved. He wishes to establish the devotion to my Immaculate Heart in the world. I promise salvation to those who embrace it; and these souls will be beloved by God like flowers arranged by me to adorn His Throne."

Opening the secret door of Mary's Immaculate Heart to grace, we can see the Throne of God. Souls who have embraced her Immaculate Heart are promised to be arrayed as flowers adorning His Throne. St. Therese of the Little Flower said, "The good God does not need years to accomplish his work of love in a soul; one ray from his heart can, in an instant, make His flower bloom for eternity..." Jesus desires to give us rays of love, to give us grace to become holy. He is working through the Immaculate Heart of Mary, transforming us to love as he loves with just one ray of love. Will you and your family enter through the secret door; receiving Jesus' rays of love to bloom as flowers into Saints and adorn the Throne of God for eternity?

TOGETHER WE PRAY...

Lord, we lift up our hearts to you, our eyes looking to you. Have mercy on us and on all souls. Open our hearts to receive your rays of love, to receive the heart of our Mother Mary, the secret door to Heaven. We thank you and we bless you! In Jesus' name we pray. Amen

FAMILY ACTIVITY

In his book, "True Devotion to Mary," St. Louis de Montfort highlights ten principal virtues of the Blessed Virgin Mary. Our eyes, on the virtues of our Heavenly Mother, will receive them into our hearts with the help of her Immaculate Heart, growing in holiness, in love, to love as God loves.

Look up St. Louis de Montfort's ten virtues of the Blessed Virgin Mary. Discuss which virtue speaks most to the heart of each family member. Write down the virtues. Seal them and place them in the tabernacle, the secret door to heaven. Pray this week, as a family, the Chaplet of the ten virtues of the Blessed Virgin Mary. Ask for her to guide your hearts and your actions, to grow in her virtues - great Saints in the making.

To you I lift up my eyes, O you who are enthroned in the Heavens! Behold, as the eyes of servants look to the hand of their master, as the eyes of a maid to the hand of her mistress, so our eyes look to the Lord our God, till he have mercy upon us. Psalm 123:1-2

CONFESSION

"God is extremely pleased by the souls that approach the great gifts of the Eucharist and the Sacrament of Confession."
— Saint Carlo Acutis

Divine rays of love and mercy, blood and water, great gifts of grace to become holy, come to us from Jesus in the Sacraments of the Eucharist and Confession, making us fully alive. Jesus transforms our souls with these rays and gifts; giving us freedom from sin, to be fully alive. Speaking to St. Faustina, Jesus said, "When you go to Confession, to this fountain of My mercy, the Blood and Water which came forth from My Heart always flows down upon your soul." Rays of Blood and Water, great gifts of grace, of life, flow down from his Heart as a fountain, pierced out of love and mercy to heal us.

The Sacrament of Confession is a Sacrament of healing. In monthly Confession, he is healing our wounded hearts. Choosing to trust him and abandon ourselves to him, by confessing our sins, he changes our sinful tendencies into virtues. He is transforming us for eternal life as his sons and daughters, right where we are placed. As a son of God, Carlo freely chose to approach the Sacrament of Confession weekly. His mother shares, "He said you have to look at the priest with eyes of faith. The confessor is like a doctor for us. In fact, it is through him that God heals the wounds which come from sin…Carlo said that through this Sacrament, it is as if a ray of light filters through the consecrated hands of the priest and tears down the shadows in which we are enveloped by sin." "My Son Carlo"

Jesus works through the priest, truly present as a Ray of Light. He told St. Faustina, "Make your confession before Me. The person of the priest is, only for Me, a screen." Approaching Jesus, fully present through the priest, we have freedom from our sins. We have the light of life, Jesus. We have the freedom to choose to see a doctor for the healing of our bodies. We have the freedom to choose to go to confession for healing of our souls, to trust in Jesus. We have the freedom to choose to love God, to fully love as he loves. God gives us this freedom to choose his Ray of Light, his love and mercy, to be fully alive. He does not force us, even if it is for our good. It is not true repentance for sin or true love, if it is forced. Monthly, by confessing and freely choosing the rays of Jesus, we will receive his healing. We become fully free of sin, a Saint fully alive where we are placed.

Even with her Immaculate Conception, Mary received from God the freedom to choose to be holy, to love as he loves. He gave her the freedom to choose to trust fully in his plan for her. He gave her the freedom to choose to remain sinless. He did not force her in any way. Authentic love and repentance from sin must be freely chosen and given from the heart. God gave Mary, from her conception, great gifts of grace, rays of light, love and mercy to be who she was meant to be, the Holy Mother of God. From her Immaculate Heart she chose to be fully alive in his gifts of grace. Every moment of every day, Mary freely chose to remain holy and free from sin. Right where she was placed, in the domestic church of her family, she remained sinless within her Immaculate Heart. Mary was fully alive with God's love. God was extremely pleased with Mary!

God was extremely pleased with how Carlo freely approached the Eucharist and the Sacrament of Confession. His soul was transformed with a fountain of mercy, rays of light, blood and water, flowing down upon his soul. St. Irenaeus is quoted saying, "The glory of God is a human being fully alive." God was glorified in Mary. She was fully alive in the domestic church of her family, free from all sin, Queen of all Saints. God was glorified in Carlo, fully alive through the transformation of his soul into a Saint. Will you and your family receive great gifts approaching the Sacrament of Confession, freely choosing to glorify God by being fully alive?

TOGETHER WE PRAY . . .

Lord, we desire to be Saints, fully alive, glorifying you with our lives. Thank you for your Divine Rays, transforming and healing our souls. We freely choose to love you; freely repenting and receiving freedom from our sins. Thank you! In Jesus' name we pray. Amen

FAMILY ACTIVITY

Carlo did not conceal his transgressions from God. He prospered on his journey of holiness. Drawn weekly to Jesus' healing power in the person of the priest, he received great gifts of grace, of life, from a Divine Fountain of Love and Mercy. Giving gifts of forgiveness, Jesus desires to give and heal all of his children, being fully alive, glorifying him.

Antonia shared that, "Carlo would recite psalm 50 [51] where King David, who repented of his sins, asks God for forgiveness." "My Son Carlo" This week, read Psalm 50 [51]. Envision King David prostrated, praying before the throne of God in his heart, with a broken and contrite heart, a heart pleasing to God. Pray together, in your hearts before the throne of God, the Divine Mercy Chaplet. Jesus, we trust in you!

He who conceals his transgressions will not prosper, but he who confesses and forsakes them will obtain mercy. Proverbs 28:13

GUARDIAN ANGEL

"Continually ask your guardian angel for help. Your guardian angel has to become your best friend." — Saint Carlo Acutis

In 1916, the year before the three shepherd children of Fatima received their first apparition of Our Lady of Fatima, an angel appeared to the children. Lucia describes the first appearance which took place shortly after they had finished praying the rosary, "This angel had the appearance of a young man of fourteen or fifteen years old, whiter than snow, which the sun rendered transparent as if it were of crystal, and of great beauty. We were surprised and half absorbed. We did not say a word. While coming closer to us, the Angel said: 'Do not fear! I am the Angel of Peace. Pray with me."

The Angel of Peace revealed to the children, in his second appearance, that he was the Guardian Angel of their country, Portugal. During the angel's third appearance, the children received the Holy Eucharist from him. Lucia received the Body of Jesus on her tongue and Francisca and Jacinta received the Precious Blood from the Chalice. Experiencing the three appearances of the Guardian Angel, were a preparation for the children to experience the six apparitions of Our Lady of Fatima in 1917.

Coming closer, the Guardian Angel of Portugal prepared the children for the journey ahead of them. His greeting, "Do not fear!," comforted them so they would not be afraid in his presence. By revealing his name to the children, "Angel of Peace," he declared his mission, peace. They were not to be anxious about surprising appearances. He asked the children to pray with him, teaching them how to seek the presence of God and his will. He served the family meal of the Holy Eucharist to the children; giving them the substance of spiritual nourishment needed for their journey to holiness, to be Saints in the holy family of God.

Coming even closer, Carlo experienced his guardian angel as his best friend, continuously asking him for help on his journey to be holy, a Saint. Giving his guardian angel the name Gabriel, he described his angel's appearance as resembling the smiling angel in France's Reims Cathedral. Antonia shares that, "Carlo was always devoted to angels. Starting when he was little, he would pray to his guardian Angel everyday and experience the concrete help that was his answer. His relationship with these messengers of God began very early," "My Son Carlo."

The Fatima children also experienced the Guardian Angel of Portugal at an early age, but our personal guardian angels greet us even earlier. At the very moment of our conception, they are given to us as a gift from God. Placed at our side for the duration of our journey to holiness, as Saints in the making, their only mission is to get us to Heaven. Praying in intercession for us and with us to God the Father, they answer our prayers with concrete help. Serving us spiritual nourishment for our journey in this relationship we build with them, they guard and protect us as we come closer to them, growing in holiness - becoming Saints.

Antonia reveals, "For Carlo, it was important to build a relationship with his guardian Angel because these faithful messengers are a special and unique gift God gives to each person. By building this personal relationship, we can benefit from his inspiration." "My Son Carlo" Will you choose to benefit from this special relationship on the journey ahead of your family and come close to your guardian angel, even as a best friend?

TOGETHER WE PRAY . . .

Prayer of the Fatima Angel Of Peace:
"My God, I believe in Thee, I adore Thee, I hope in Thee and I love Thee. I ask pardon for all those who do not believe in Thee, do not adore Thee, do not hope in Thee and do not love Thee."

FAMILY ACTIVITY

Each of our guardian angels is a unique gift from God's goodness, mercy and love. They desire to build a personal relationship with us, as best friends, that will exist for all of eternity in Heaven. Taking time to pray to them, by requesting and relying on their help, we receive inspiration and answers, according to God's will, that are always for our good, as they love as God loves.

Start building your families eternal friendship with their guardian angels. Pray daily, writing down on narrow slips of paper, your prayers and requests, those for yourself and for others. Construct a prayer chain with each slip, each prayer, connecting to the others. Continue on your journey to pray, construct, and connect with your angel and with each other. Return periodically, giving thanks to your guardian angel for how they have answered your prayers. Thank God for his special gift of your guardian angel.

See that you do not despise one of these little ones, for I tell you that in Heaven their angels always behold the Face of my Father who is in Heaven. Matthew 18:10

HOLY FACE DEVOTION

"If we go out in the sun, we get a suntan...but when we get in front of Jesus in the Eucharist, we become saints."

— Saint Carlo Acutis

During Eucharistic Adoration, the veiled Eucharistic Face of Jesus Christ shines forth from the Blessed Sacrament, the Sacrament of his Love. We are worshipping him, truly present in front of us. We are adoring the Real Presence of Jesus, his Body, Blood, Soul and Divinity really, truly, substantially present in the consecrated Host. From his place in the Monstrance, Jesus is showering upon us rays of light, of grace, of love. Sitting before the Eucharistic Presence of Jesus, we bask in the rays coming forth from the very heart of the glorious Son of God, hidden in the Host, becoming holy, Saints loving as he loves.

Pope St. John Paul II was the first to use the term, "Eucharistic Face of Christ." In preparation for dedicating the third millennium to the "Radiant sign of the Face of Christ," he had earlier commissioned an International Congress to study the Devotion to the Holy Face and Holy Face medal. Both were approved by Pope Pius XII in 1958. Pope St. John Paul II promoted daily Eucharistic Adoration. On April 17, 2003, he said, "Adoration of the Blessed Sacrament is...an important daily practice and becomes an inexhaustible source of holiness...it is pleasant to spend time with (Christ), to lie close to his breast like the beloved disciple and to feel the infinite love present in His Heart."

Carlo basked in front of the hidden Eucharistic Face of Jesus as often as he could, spending time worshipping him and receiving rays of love from his heart. He said, "Jesus is very creative because he hides in a little piece of bread, and only God could do something so incredible!" He compared his time at Eucharistic Adoration to lying incredibly close to the Heart of Jesus. Carlo had been inspired by the meal of the Last Supper where, "One of his disciples, whom Jesus loved, was lying close to the breast of Jesus." (John 13:23) Carlo was a beloved disciple of Jesus. He felt the infinite love of Jesus, heart to heart at Eucharistic Adoration. Carlo leaned on the very heart, the very breast of the Eucharistic Jesus, just as St. John did before the institution of the Eucharist. Jesus lives and works in the Eucharist, in incredibly, creative ways that only he can do, making Saints!

We are all called to possess what Carlo described as, "Eucharistic souls in which God works those marvels in us that only he can do." Carlo said, "Conversion is nothing other than turning one's gaze away from the inferior to the superior. It takes nothing more than diverting our eyes to another direction." We need to divert our gaze to the Holy Face of Jesus. We need to change direction and focus on him, being totally devoted to his Holy Face, veiled in the Eucharist. Working marvels, Jesus is an inexhaustible source of holiness in Eucharistic Adoration. Gazing upon him and worshipping before him, he becomes an inexhaustible source of holiness, of infinite love felt from his heart.

"To contemplate the Face of Christ, and to contemplate it with Mary, is the program which I have set before the Church at the dawn of the third millennium," Pope St. John Paul II. As the domestic church, spend time contemplating the Face of Christ with Mary, gazing upon the Eucharistic Face of Jesus in Adoration. In devotion with the Immaculate Heart of Mary, contemplate his Holy Face, praying the Chaplet of the Holy Face with your family. With Mary, Saint Carlo Acutis and St. John contemplate his Holy Face, his heart of infinite love, resting the Holy Face medal upon your heart, your chest, as his beloved disciple. "He is always looking at you; can you not turn the eyes of your soul and look at him?" St Teresa of Avila. How will you turn the eyes of your family to contemplate the Holy Face of Jesus?

TOGETHER WE PRAY . . .

Lord, Praise, honor and Glory to you, present in the Sacrament of your love, your Eucharistic Face, which shines upon us in love. We thank you, we bless you, we adore you, basking in your rays of light and love, for making us holy. We pray in the name of Jesus, contemplating his Holy Face. Amen

FAMILY ACTIVITY

Feel the infinite love of Jesus who is an inexhaustible source of holiness, light, love and grace. Have your family, as his beloved disciples, lean upon his breast. At an adoration chapel, sit in the presence of the Eucharistic Face of the Lord of Heaven and earth. He is the King of Love, veiled in the Sacrament of his love. He will make you a Saint!

The Holy Face Devotion is a prayer of reparation to God for the sins of blasphemy, atheism, abortion, communism, and the profanation of Sunday and Holy Days of obligation. St. Therese of Lisieux was deeply devoted to the Holy Face of Jesus. She said, "O Jesus! Your veiled gaze is our Heaven!" Daily pray the "Golden Arrow" prayer this week and become deeply devoted to his Holy Face.

The Lord bless you and keep you. The Lord make his Face shine upon you, and be gracious to you. The Lord turn his face toward you, and give you peace

Numbers 6:24-26

4TH SATURDAY | WEEK 4

OUR LADY OF POMPEII

"After the Holy Eucharist, the Holy Rosary is the most powerful weapon for fighting the devil and the shortest ladder for climbing into Heaven."
— Saint Carlo Acutis

Appearing to all three shepherd children, for the sixth and final apparition on October 13th, 1917, Our Lady of Fatima fulfilled her promise to reveal to them who she was. She announced, "I am the Lady of the Rosary. Continue to pray the rosary every day." Opening her hands she dispatched a ray of light in the direction of the sun. Lucia shouted to the people gathered; pointing to the sun. It was then, that the promised sign for everyone to believe took place, the miracle of the sun.

Lucia continued to point throughout her long life to Our Lady of the Rosary and the importance of daily praying the Rosary. In a letter to Mother Martins from September 1970, published in 2021 by Soul Magazine, she promoted the Rosary as a powerful weapon for our times, saying, "The Most Holy Virgin in these last times in which we live has given a new efficacy to the recitation of the rosary to such an extent that there is no problem, no matter how difficult it is, whether temporal or above all spiritual, in the personal life of each one of us, of our families...that cannot be solved by the Rosary."

Pointing to the importance of families daily praying the Rosary, Pope St. John Paul II professed, "How beautiful is the family that recites the Rosary every evening." Stating that, "The Rosary is my favorite prayer," he declared the rosary, "as a genuine training in holiness... destined to bring about a harvest of holiness."

Pope St. John Paul II was convinced that our families needed the efficacious power of this ladder of holiness, this weapon, for climbing into Heaven as Saints.

Saint Carlo Acutis realized the importance of daily praying the Rosary to become a Saint. He had a deep devotion to the Most Holy Virgin and the Rosary saying, "The Virgin Mother is the only woman in my life...I never fail to keep the most gracious appointment of the day - recitation of the Holy Rosary." His mother, Antonia, shares in, "My Son Carlo," about his deep devotion, "Over the course of his life, we had performed seven acts of entrustment to Our Lady of Pompeii, who is Our Lady of the Rosary, with a powerful blessing from a priest." Carlo, in entrusting himself to Our Lady of Pompeii, she became his weapon, his shortest ladder to climbing into Heaven as a Saint!

The Blessed Mother, as Our Lady of Pompeii, represents Our Lady of the Rosary as Queen of Heaven. She is also known as Our Lady of Victory, after the decisive Battle of Lepanto on Oct. 7th, 1571. Pope St. Pius V ordered the Churches of Rome to be kept open day and night for the faithful to pray for victory over the Turks. The faithful, by praying the Rosary, in petition for the intercession of the Blessed Virgin, won the battle with a most powerful weapon, a warrior Queen, Our Lady of Victory. Pope St. Pius V set the Feast day of her victory as October 7th, now the Feast of the Holy Rosary.

We have a victorious Queen of Heaven, the Mother of God, a most powerful warrior Queen! She is a Mighty General in her Son's Army! She fights for our holiness, as our own Mother, a Mother who never tires or grows weary. A Mother who loves us as God loves us. She is the most powerful weapon, the shortest ladder for all to climb into Heaven as Saints. Pope St. John Paul II urged all to pray the Rosary saying, "May this appeal of mine not go unheard!" Let us all heed his call, may it not go unheard! Sister Lucia ended her letter to Mother Martins with her own call for the Immaculate Heart to triumph in our hearts with the Rosary, "Let us pray, work and sacrifice and trust that finally, 'my Immaculate Heart will triumph.'" May the Immaculate Heart of Mary triumph in Victory in our hearts, that we all may love as God loves, becoming holy! May we all climb into Heaven, on the shortest ladder of the Holy Rosary, as Saints, royal sons and daughters of God the Father, one Holy Family of Love! Amen

TOGETHER WE PRAY . . .

Lord, we come before you, praying for a harvest of holiness in all our families. We ask for the Immaculate Heart of Mary to be victorious in every heart, all your royal sons and daughters loving as you love — the greatest of Saints. Thank you for hearing our prayers. In Jesus' name we pray. Amen

FAMILY ACTIVITY

In praying the most powerful of weapons — the rosary, miracles, temporal and spiritual, take place! Our Lady of the Rosary, sends rays of light, pointing to her Son, for all souls to go to Heaven. Consecrated to the Immaculate Heart of Mary, we climb the shortest ladder to Heaven, rung by rung in the refuge of Our Lady of Victory to be the greatest of Saints!

Thank the Blessed Mother for being your family's weapon for holiness — to love as God loves. Together, pray the Glorious Mysteries on mariavision.us with the children's video. Create a crown, embellishing it with love from the heart. In a family procession, place the crown upon the Tabernacle placed on the altar. Enthrone Our Lady of Pompeii, consecrating the hearts of your family to our Mother, the Queen of Heaven and Earth.

And he came to her and said, Hail, full of grace, the Lord is with you!
Luke 1:28

WEEKLY CHALLENGE

St. Joseph, foster father of Jesus and patron Saint of families and workers, was an ordinary man, working an ordinary job. Living in an ordinary way, he experienced the stress and challenges of everyday life. The difference was his response. St. Joseph responded to the call to be holy, by being protector and provider of Jesus and Mary. He served them and his neighbor with extraordinary love. Called to be holy, extraordinary in love, each unique Saint lives their ordinary life. In extraordinary ways, they respond by loving and serving those around them, filled with love for God and their neighbor.

Being a Saint is not for people of the past in an easier age. The time to be a Saint is right here, right now! There are many millennials in the Catholic Church currently on their way to canonization. Their lives are an inspiration for our own journey.

Each week, research the person listed and their path to Sainthood. Learn how they exemplified holiness, love for God and neighbor. Explore the Vatican Approved Eucharistic Miracles and Marian Apparitions; experienced by ordinary people, living ordinary lives. Share your findings with your family. Together, journey to victory with Saint Joseph, he is a Warrior King, and be a Saint!

	HOLY IN LOVE	EUCHARISTIC MIRACLE	MARIAN APPARITION	PRAY
1ST SATURDAY	Servant of God Pierangelo Capuzzimati, Taranto, Italy (1990-2008)	Trani, Italy, Eleventh Century	Diocesan Shrine Rosa Mystica, Mother of the Church, Italy ~ Our Lady of Montichiari	Litany of Loreto
WEEK 2	Servant of God Sister Clare Crockett, Derry, Northern Ireland (1982- 2016)	Legnica, Poland, Christmas Day, 2013	National Eucharistic and Marian Shrine of Knock, Ireland ~ Our Lady of Knock	Litany of Our Lady of Knock
WEEK 3	Venerable Matteo Farina, Avellino, Italy (1990-2009)	Scala, Italy September 11th, 1732	Pontifical Shrine of the Blessed Virgin of the Rosary of Pompeii, Italy ~ Our Lady of Pompeii	Litany of Our Lady of Pompeii
WEEK 4	Servant of God Helena Agnieszka Kmiec, Krakow, Poland (1991-2017)	Sokolka, Poland, October 12th, 2008	National Shrine of Our Lady of Czestochowa, Poland ~ Black Madonna	Litany of the Black Madonna
2ND SATURDAY	Servant of God Akash Bashir, Risalpur, Pakistan (1994-2015)	Ludbreg, Croatia, 1411	National Marian Shrine of Mariamabad, Pakistan ~ "City of Mary"	Litany of the Holy Family
WEEK 2	Servant of God Jean Thierry Ebogo, Bamenda, Cameroon (1982-2006)	Saint-André De La Reunion, January 26th, 1902	Our Lady of Banneux, Belgium ~ Virgin of the Poor	Litany of the Holy Face of Jesus
WEEK 3	Servant of God Floribert Bwana Choi bin Kositi, Goma, Republic Congo (1981-2007)	Etan, Peru, June 2nd, and July 22nd, 1649	Saydet Bechwat Ancient Church, Lebanon ~ Our Lady of Bechwat	Litany of the Most Holy Trinity
WEEK 4	Servant of God Father Ragheed Aziz Ganni, Mosul, Iraq (1972-2007)	Skete, Egypt, third-fifth centuries	Our Lady of Zeitoun, Egypt ~ Our Lady of Light.	Litany of the Holy Innocents
3RD SATURDAY	Servant of God Anne-Gabrielle Caron, Toulon, France (2002-2010)	La Rochelle, France, during Easter, 1461	Our Lady of Pontmain, France ~ Our Lady of Hope	Litany of Hope
WEEK 2	Servant of God Giulia Gabrieli, Bergamo, Italy (1997-2011)	Gruaro (Valvasone), Italy, 1294 AD	Our Lady of Medjugorje, Bosnia-Herzegovina ~ Mother of the Redeemer	Litany of Peace
WEEK 3	Servant of God Darwin Ramos, Pasay, Philippines (1994-2012)	Morne-Rouge, Caribbean Island of Martinique, May 8th, 1902	Shrine of Our Lady of Montligeon, France ~ Our Lady of Liberatrix	Litany for the Holy Souls in Purgatory
WEEK 4	Servant of God Chiara Corbella Petrillo, Rome, Italy (1984-2012)	Bolsena, Italy, 1263	Tre Fontane, Rome, Italy ~ The Virgin of Revelation	Litany of Assumption of Blessed Virgin Mary
4TH SATURDAY	Saint Pier Giorgio Frassati, Turin, Italy (1901-1925)	Turin, Italy, 1453	Pontifical Church and Marian Shrine, Turin, Italy ~ Our Lady, Help of Christians	Litany of Blessed Virgin Mary
WEEK 2	Blessed Chiara Bandano, Sassello, Italy (1971-1990)	Betania, Venezuela, December 8th, 1991	Betania, Venezuela ~ Our Lady of Betania ~ "Reconciler of Peoples and Nations"	Litany on Behalf of Our Country
WEEK 3	Servant of God Michelle Duppong, Wheat Ridge, CO, USA, (1984-2015)	Valencia, Spain ~ The Holy Grail of Valencia	National Shrine of Our Lady of Champion, WI, USA ~ Our Lady of Champion	Litany of Our Lady of Victory
WEEK 4	Saint Carlo Acutis, Milan, Italy (1991-2006)	Tixtla, Mexico, October 21st, 2006	Tepeyac, Mexico ~ Our Lady of Guadelupe	Litany in Honor of Jesus, King of All Nations

CERTIFICATE
OF CONSECRATION

Most Holy Virgin Mary,

tender Mother of men, to fulfill the desires of the Sacred Heart of Jesus and the request of the Vicar of Your Son on earth, we consecrate ourselves and our families to your Sorrowful and Immaculate Heart, O Queen of the Most Holy Rosary, and we recommend to You, all the people of our country and all the world.

Please accept our consecration, dearest Mother, and use us as You wish to accomplish Your designs in the world.

O Sorrowful and Immaculate Heart of Mary, Queen of the Most Holy Rosary, and Queen of the World, rule over us, together with the Sacred Heart of Jesus Christ, Our King. Save us from the spreading flood of modern paganism; kindle in our hearts and homes the love of purity, the practice of a virtuous life, an ardent zeal for souls, and a desire to pray the Rosary more faithfully.

We come with confidence to You, O Throne of Grace and Mother of Fair Love. Inflame us with the same Divine Fire which has inflamed Your own Sorrowful and Immaculate Heart. Make our hearts and homes Your shrine, and through us, make the Heart of Jesus, together with your rule, triumph in every heart and home.

Amen

_____

Parent(s) Signature

_____

Child(ren) Signature

_____

Priest/Deacon Signature

A NOTE FROM THE AUTHOR

Thank you to my amazing friends, Judy Brown and Cecilia Lehman. They were both inspirations for me; helped me to edit, and encouraged and supported me on the journey, keeping me focused on the mission at hand. Thank you to my wonderful friends, Cathy Lien, Jo Ann Kleekamp and Carolyn Martin who have fully supported me from the beginning. They have given graciously of themselves and their time to help teach the Real Presence and share about Saint Carlo Acutis. Thank you to my generous friend Lucille Sherry, who persistently hunted for the treasure of Holy Family Devotions in the Domestic Church, for our families to grow in holiness.

Thank you Traci Douglass, for gifting us with the use of your beautiful, tender, loving original image of Jesus, "Lo, I Am With You Always." Thank you George and Polly Capps, for creating the incredible, original piece of Sacred Art for the family consecration movement, "Be A Saint In the Making!" Thank you to Colleen Sneed, her beautiful gifts of graphic design and patience, have given this workbook and everything she has worked on for the Real Presence, a beauty that points to God!

Thank you Father Charles Archer for always supporting me, taking the time to be available to guide me on this journey! Thank you to my husband, Brian, and my family! I am so very grateful for your patience and generosity of spirit as I took time to write, whenever and wherever I could. I love you! Thank you Guardian Angels, for always protecting us and loving us on our journey home, as Saints in the making. Thank you to the Holy Spirit, this is His work. It was truly inspired with the fire of love, from the Hearts of Jesus, Mary and Joseph, and mine from within theirs. God the Father, thank you for bringing your love into our homes, the Domestic Church, making us Saints!

Thank you to the family of Saint Carlo Acutis, for sharing him with everyone. Thank you Saint Carlo Acutis, for the blessing of sharing your life's journey with us and interceding for us on our own journey to be Saints. Thank you Saint Joseph, for protecting our families, as you protected Mary and Jesus, as the first Holy Family. We are all blessed to be part of your Holy Family. Thank you Blessed Mother, for the refuge of Your Immaculate Heart and walking with us, as our Mother, on our journey home to your Son, our Lord and Savior, Jesus Christ! To all my brothers and sisters in Jesus Christ, thank you for joining this journey, as a family, God's Holy Family of Love!

*God's blessings and love for you and your family on your journey to **"Be Saints in the Making!"***

Kristi Dentinger

REAL PRESENCE EDUCATION FOUNDATION

REAL PRESENCE
Education Foundation
Witnessing God's Love in the Eucharist

January: The Holy Name of Jesus

February: The Holy Family

March: Saint Joseph - Annunciation (Saint Patrick)

April: The Holy Spirit

May: The Blessed Virgin Mary

June: The Sacred Heart of Jesus

July: The Precious Blood of Jesus

August: The Immaculate Heart of Mary

September: The Seven Sorrows of Mary

October: Our Lady of the Rosary (Saint Carlo Acutis)

November: The Holy Souls in Purgatory (All Saints)

December: Immaculate Conception and Birth of Christ (Saint Nicholas and Others)

Celebrating, joyously, as the Holy Family of God the Father:
Easter - the Resurrection of our Lord and Savior (40 days from Ash Wednesday)
Pentecost - the Birthday of the Church, the Holy Family of God the Father
(50 days from Christ's Resurrection, the 7th Sunday of Easter)

⊛ENROUTE
Make the time

www.ingramcontent.com/pod-product-compliance
Lightning Source LLC
Chambersburg PA
CBHW061049090426

42740CB00002B/96